AN ILLUSTRATED
HISTORY OF
DERBYSHIRE

AN ILLUSTRATED HISTORY OF
DERBYSHIRE

JOHN HEATH

The Breedon Books
Publishing Company
Derby

First published in Great Britain by
The Breedon Books Publishing Company Limited
44 Friar Gate, Derby DE1 1DA
1993

ISBN 1 873626 37 1

Printed and bound by Hillmans Printers, Frome, Somerset.
Cover printed by BDC Printing Services Ltd of Derby.
Cover photographs by Andy Williams.

Contents

Illustration Acknowledgements

Aerofilms — 111 (bottom)

Arkwright Society — 73

Stuart Band — 97 (right)

Cambridge University Collection — 8 (top), 15, 16, (left), 18, 21, 23, 25, 26, 33, 35, 38, 41, 43, 54 (top left), 55 (bottom), 63, 109.

W.A.Camwell — 97 (left).

A.E.Harrison Collection — 99, 112

Fred Hartley — 20, 51 (bottom) 75, 129.

John Heath Collection — 11, 26 (bottom), 28, 30, 39, 48, 52, 54 , 55 (top), 56, 59, 62, 64, 68, 69, 71, 72, 76, 79, 81, 83 (top), 84 (left), 85 (bottom), 86, 88, 89, 90, 92, 93, 94, 96 (top), 98, 99 (top), 100, 103, 104, 105, 106, 107, 111 (top), 112, 114 (top), 115 (right) 119, 121.

Trustees of the British Museum — 87.

Derek Riley — 33 (top)

Frank Rodgers — 8, 9, 12, 14, 15 (bottom), 16 (boittom), 20 (bottom) 25, 29, 34, 36, 37, 40, 42, 44, 45, 50, 53, 54 (top right), 55, 57, 58, 74, 76 (top), 77, 78, 80, 83, 84 (right), 90 (top), 91, 110, 114, 115 (left), 116, 117, 124, 126, 127, 128.

Royal Commission on the Historical Monuments of England — 15 (top), 16 (right).

Victoria and Albert Museums, Mowat Collection — 67, 94 (top).

Andy Williams — Cover photographs.

Richard Winstone — 46, 85, 86 (right), 96 (centre right).

Dedication
To Joyce

Introduction

PUBLISHED a decade ago, this book was written for the student, teacher or general reader searching for an introduction to the history of Derbyshire. In those ten years, more material has become available, both in primary and secondary sources. Where possible I have corrected mistakes and amended and added to the text as well as adding to the pictorial coverage.

In writing the book I began by looking at events in a roughly chronological sequence. However, the increased range of activities which have evolved during the past three centuries led me to look at that period thematically, as any attempt to interlink the many themes would be confusing. Inevitably, as a result of this dual approach, there is a duplication of material.

The maps and diagrams have been compiled from original work, although some naturally replicate illustrations that have appeared elsewhere. In the main they are an adjunct to the text and with the pictures should be viewed in conjunction with it.

I would like to acknowledge advice freely given by Dudley Fowkes, Keith Challis and Evelyn Lord, and to the many colleagues and friends who have unwittingly contributed to my Derbyshire awareness. However, errors of interpretation are solely mine.

Genesis

There are prospects in Derbyshire as noble as any in Greece or Switzerland. Byron

WITHIN the boundaries of Derbyshire there is a variety of scenery ranging from the inhospitable gritstone plateaus of the High Peak, to the gently rolling open landscape of the Trent lowlands in the south.

In the north and west of the County the wild, heatherclad gritstone moorlands and edges of Kinder Scout and Axe Edge rise to about 600 metres above sea-level. To the south of these moorlands is the rounded upland landscape of the mountain limestone, a green pastureland, criss-crossed by stone walls and dissected by the deep cut gorges of the Wye, Dove and Lathkill rivers. Both of these areas and the intervening softer shale country which is followed by the River Derwent, have been and are being exploited by man, but in no way have they suffered from the hand of man as have the coal measures of the eastern portion of the County — a landscape scarred with slag-heaps, opencast workings, and the associated paraphernalia of industrial activity.

Yet even in this part of Derbyshire there are patches of open country and small parklands, reminders of the prosperous land-owning yeoman of yesteryear and the extensive woodlands which once covered the area. However, as the years pass, the despoiled landscape is being effectively camouflaged by nature, and reclaimed by man.

In the southern part of the County, wide, open valleys, meadowland and man-made parkland are found on the more easily eroded sandstones and

Looking towards Kinder Scout and the Downfall.

Looking from the Downfall to the Kinder Reservoir.

Dovedale — a limestone gorge.

marls which are often overlain with glacial and alluvial deposits. By contrast, on the borders of Leicestershire a coal measure and limestone landscape reappears.

With such a variety of rock-type, it is little wonder that there is a wide range of domestic building styles. Timber buildings, both cruck and box frame, are to be found mainly in the Trent and lower Dove and Derwent valleys and their tributaries, but few remain in the uplands.

Timber-framed building was traditional in the northern portion of the County before the sixteenth century, and persisted in the south well into the seventeenth century, examples of either cruck or box-frame structures standing in most villages. This accords with William Harrison's observation in 1588 that 'The greatest part of our building in the cities and good towns of England, consisteth only of timber, for as yet few houses of the Commonalty . . .are made of stone . . .'

However, Derbyshire towns and villages did not experience the devastating fires found elsewhere in the Kingdom. Many of the large timbers from the earlier buildings appear to have been re-used, with eighteenth

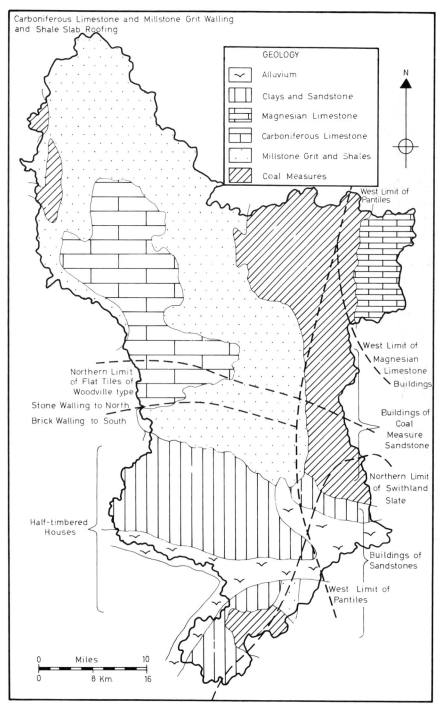

The basic geology and building materials.

century buildings incorporating timbers at least one hundred years older than the structure.

The great re-build of the seventeenth century was still dependent upon local materials, local stone, local-fired bricks and red tiles, although thatch was used until the eighteenth century, as is evidenced in the steeply pitched gables. In the north, stone slates, obtained locally, were used in the sixteenth and seventeenth centuries, resulting in flatter roofs. In the south, Swithland slates and blue tiles replaced the thatch. The stone houses of the sixteenth century are often gabled on all sides, but the seventeenth century style appears to revert to a simple box-shaped, fairly square house, with a central door and chimney.

Although most of the County must have been subjected to glacial activity, Derbyshire does not have extensive areas of landscape smothered with glacial deposits, nor does it have upland which bears the marks of ice-scouring. There are boulder clay deposits in various parts of the County, and there are erratics in the

Buxton area, but the most important glacial deposits are the fluvio-glacial terraces laid down in association with the glacial lakes which were ponded back by the ice-sheets. These terraces are some of the more important gravel resources which are being exploited today.

Several of the rivers of the County have been dammed to provide valuable drinking water. Patrick Monkhouse in *On Foot in the Peak* (1932) wrote 'There is not a stream running west from these moors which is not dammed somewhere, excepting only Black Brook at Chinley'.

The Derwent Valley Water Board was established in 1899 for the purpose of reconciling the water demands of the three large neighbouring urban areas — Sheffield, Leicester and Nottingham — and the County of Derby. The Howden and Derwent reservoirs were completed in 1912 and the Ladybower dam was opened by George VI in 1945. These areas of water, along with those in the Goyt and Longdendale valleys, and at Ogston, Foremark and Carsington, have considerably modified the landscape.

In considering the Derbyshire scene it is important to bear in mind the variations in climate that are experienced within the County area. The upland areas receive an average of one hundred and fifty centimetres of snow and rainfall annually, and there are approximately forty days when snow can be expected.

By comparison the lowlands of the Trent receive as little as sixty centimetres a year. In a normal year the south-east can expect fifty more hours of sunshine than the area around Buxton, where snow is a winter hazard. Buxton can be the coldest and wettest place in Europe! Aspect is important to man's activities. In the northern valleys, in particular the Edale Valley, the difference between north and south-facing slopes is crucial to settlement and to agricultural activities.

The date when man first came to Derbyshire is not known. He must have arrived in the area about 30,000 years ago during the last stages of the Great Ice Age. The only tool that this early man had was a pear-shaped stone axe, examples of which are found in the gravel deposits of the river Trent at Hilton, and in the vicinity of Barrow-on-Trent. These early men lived a nomadic existence dependent upon the killing of animals. Alongside the axes are frequently found the bones of rhinoceros, hippopotamus, elephant and sabre-toothed tiger. This period is known as the Palaeolithic.

Other early settlers in the Palaeolithic period lived permanently in caves in the Carboniferous Limestone, as at Harborough near Brassington, and in the Magnesian Limestone at Whaley and Creswell Crags, where the short river-cut gorge contains twenty-four caves and rock shelters. In Pinhole Cave at Creswell Crags there is evidence which suggests that man had to leave his caves because of flooding, possibly associated with one of the warmer interglacial periods.

Excavations of the caves have revealed household rubbish, discarded tools, the bones of animals and the relics of hearths, indicating that cavemen used fire for warmth and cooking. His implements, which show evidence of pressure-flaking, were made of quartzite, instead of flint which is scarce in the East Midlands, and reindeer antlers were made into picks. Bones of animals excavated include those of giant deer, wild horses, bison and lions. Other layers include bones of the mammoth, the cave hyena, the woolly rhinoceros, bison and the lemming, which suggest a period when a colder climate prevailed.

The Palaeolithic period came to an end with the Mesolithic period when microliths were commonly used. These flints are under half an inch in length, and when hafted in a row, make spears or harpoons. Quantitites of these flints are to be found in the higher areas, particularly on Bleaklow and Stanage Edge. Other than the flints there is little evidence of Mesolithic man.

Neolithic man, with his improved technology, appears in Britain about four thousand years ago. Like his predecessors, he lived in caves as at Longcliffe, near Brassington, and in simple huts. He fashioned round-bottomed clay pots,

The cruck beams of Kilburn tithe barn.

A typical Peak District house of the seventeeth century with grit quoins, lintels and mullions, limestone and shaley grit roofing slates.

Ladybower Reservoir looking south.

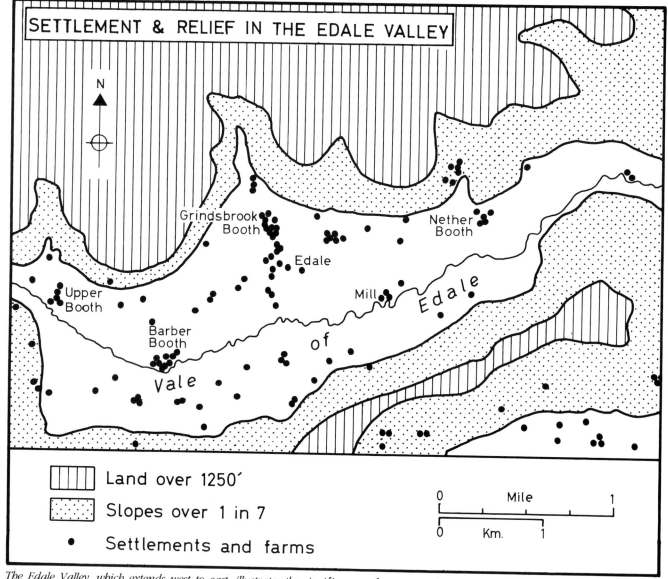

SETTLEMENT & RELIEF IN THE EDALE VALLEY

N

Grindsbrook
Booth

Edale

Nether
Booth

Upper
Booth

Mill

Edale

Barber
Booth

of

Vale

Land over 1250′

Slopes over 1 in 7

• Settlements and farms

0   Mile   1

0   Km.   1

The Edale Valley, which extends west to east, illustrates the significance of aspect and slope to the siting of settlements and farms in upland areas. North-facing slopes have no settlements and few farms. The steepness of the slope may be a deterrent. Inhabitants of Castleton walked daily across Mam Tor ridge to work in the Edale cotton mill, enlarged from a corn mill in 1795. Cotton manufacturing ceased in 1934.

Near Taddington.

Sites associated with pre-Roman settlement.

Avebury, stands on a circular mound 250 feet (76 metres) in diameter within which is a ditch, the limestone slabs lying flat. Gibb Hill, another artificial mound, lies outside the Arbor Low circle, and resembles a miniature Silbury Hill. There is another monument of exactly the same dimensions located at Dove Holes, near Buxton. This is called the Bull Ring, but there are no stone slabs on the site, which poses one of its many questions. It is intriguing to speculate on the labour force involved in the construction of these henges and tombs, bearing in mind the few crude tools that were then available. To the south of Derby, two cursus (Aston and Potlock) suggest an important ceremonial centre.

Bronze Age man's technology gradually supplanted that of Neolithic man. He appears to have mingled peacefully with his predecessors, introducing them to more sophisticated tools. Stone hammers were holed for ease of hafting and bronze knives were made, although the metal was a scarce commodity. The Nine Ladies on Stanton Moor is made up of gritstone blocks standing no more than three feet (one metre) out of the ground. There is a single block outside the ring called the King Stone, which would appear to be similar in function to Gibb Hill. Another circle of this period stands on Harthill Moor, and both circles have graves within them.

Bronze Age burial mounds are small and round. In them Bronze Age man interred his dead, while those who arrived later practised cremation, the remains being placed in earthenware pots. Over the small stone-slabbed chamber, in which the body or pot was placed, was mounded earth some six feet (1.8 metres) high and sixty feet (18 metres) in diameter. There are at least seventy of these burial mounds on Stanton Moor. While the Neolithic burial mounds contained multiple burials, all those of the Bronze Age were individual. The distribution of the mounds or barrows shows the body barrows to be on the highest areas of the limestone country, while the cremations are sited chiefly on lower-lying gritstone areas.

Iron Age man's technology

leaf-shaped spears of finely chipped flints, and adzes which were made out of any available fine-grained rock which could be highly polished by sand and water, a technique which distinguishes Neolithic from Palaeolithic man. These people practised a simple type of arable agriculture and kept cattle and sheep. A Neolithic settlement excavated at Lismore Fields — Buxton — revealed two post-built rectangular buildings, pottery, flint tools, and charred seed and plant remains

including wheat, flax, hazel nuts and crab apples.

Two large-scale works that Neolithic man has left behind are tombs and stone circles. There are several tombs, of which Five Wells Tumulus, standing on a cliff of Mountain Limestone overlooking the river Wye near Taddington, is the best example of a passage grave. Formerly covered by an earth mound 56 feet (17 metres) in diameter, it contained at least twelve skeletons. Arbor Low, near Parsley Hay, a henge monument like

Two Neolithic chambered tombs at Minninglow, excavated by Thomas Bateman.

Arbor Low.

extended into Derbyshire about seven centuries before the coming of the Romans. Below Robin Hood's Stride and in Demon's Dale near Taddington, remains of their villages have been found. Bone and iron articles abound as well as varied shapes of pottery. Iron Age man kept animals and used horses as beasts of burden. Querns, or hand mills, indicate that he ate much grain, some of which was grown on fields delimited on their lower sides by scarps or lynchets usually located at valley heads, examples of which are to be found in the vicinity of Priestcliffe, Taddington, Alsop-en-le-dale, Youlgreave and Bakewell.

Iron Age man settled throughout the area, leaving evidence at Ball Cross near Bakewell and Harbo-

Aerial view of Arbor Low and Gibb Hill. The walled fields of the nineteenth century are broken by dew ponds.

Oblique view of the Bull Ring henge monument at Dove Holes. Bottom left is the scar of quarrying.

rough Rocks near Brassington. He later constructed defensive positions for retreat and shelter from raiding neighbours. He built Castle Ring on Harthill Moor, a fort on Mam Tor, Fin Cop above Monsal Dale, Combs Moss at Whaley Bridge, and Markland Grips near Elmton. One of the most impressive examples is Carl Wark on Burbage Moor above Hathersage, which uses a natural platform with three sides, almost perpendicular, and with the fourth side protected by a massive wall of gritstone blocks.

In the Iron Age, lowland Derbyshire appears to have been densely occupied by small farming communities, rectangular cropmark enclosures identifying the sites. At Swarkestone, to the west of the Barrows, a cluster of such communities indicates a possible small town. Excavations, ahead of the gravel extractors and the motorway builders, are revealing more and more evidence of prehistoric settlement in all parts of lowland Derbyshire.

The Nine Ladies, Stanton Moor.

An oblique view of Mam Tor showing the landslips of shale rock which pre-date the Iron Age fort. The single rampart and ditch enclose an area of about sixteen acres. Within this are two Bronze Age barrows and several hut sites.

Carl Wark.

The hill top which overlooks the Wye Valley is the site of the Iron Age fort — Fin Cop.

The Incomers

THE extension of Rome's frontiers to include Britain took place in the years after AD 43, following the Roman conquest of France (Gaul) between 58 and 50 BC. Occupation was a gradual process with the Romans meeting increasing resistance from the Celts, the Iron Age tribes, who were forced to retreat to the highland fastnesses or accept Roman rule. The Peak, from Pecsaetan (Old English term meaning 'peak dwellers' coined in Tribal Hidage in the eighth century), was an area of conflict between civilian and military Britain. The Romans reached the Trent about AD 47 and consolidated their occupation of south-east England with a temporary frontier marked by the Fosse Way. To the north were the Coritani and Brigantes tribes. The occupation of the area between the Trent and the Don took place between AD 50 and 70, during which time they built an advanced fort, overlooking a crossing-point on the River Derwent in the area known today as Strutt's Park.

Having gained control of the north, the fort was dismantled and the Romans established a garrison on the east bank of the Derwent crossing with an adjacent civilian service settlement which included kilns. Archaeologists have identified six phases of settlement on the Little Chester site. The occupation troops were largely recruited from the Provinces of Rome and some would have had a kinship with the Britons. The fort at Little Chester, the Roman *Derventio*, commanded the point on the Derwent where the roads from Cirencester and Wall (Rykneld Way), from Chester, Chesterton and the fort

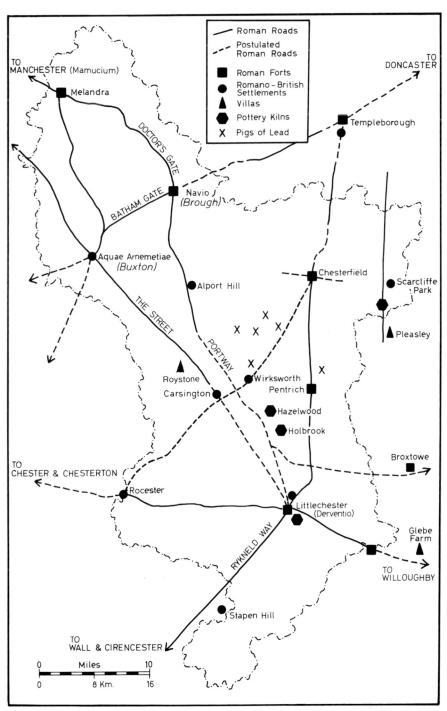

The main sites of the Roman occupation of Derbyshire between c.AD 55 and c.AD 380. Roman roads had varied surfaces. Batham Gate and Rykneld Way were built on raised causeways but in the Holbrook area, coal was used to surface the road.

17

Aerial view of the site of Melandra Castle, the Roman fort built on a spur of land projecting into the Etherow Valley. Built c.AD 78 like Brough, it suffered from frequent attacks by the Brigantes. The original clay rampart was reinforced after AD 100 by a stone wall with gateways, which enclosed an area of five acres. Within the walls were buildings including wooden barracks. A civilian settlement was sited to the east and south-east of the fort. The fort was of strategic importance guarding the Woodhead and Snake Passes as well as the route to Manchester from Buxton and the east.

at Rocester, from the crossing point over the Trent near Sawley, from the forts at Chesterfield and Temple-borough, and from Aquae Arneme-tiae, (the baths at Buxton), met and crossed the river. These Roman roads either followed pre-historic track-ways or were built in straight lines across the countryside, the Romans taking into account the lie of the land and the prevailing weather, so that it is not often that a stretch of Roman road is blocked by snow.

In the highland part of the County, two forts were built to contain the hill people of the Peak as well as administering the lead industry. The Navio or Brough fort was built at an important river crossing, and at a junction in the strategic network of roads which crossed the Peak. Navio was linked with Buxton by Batham Gate on which the sole Roman milestone in Derbyshire was found, with Melandra Castle (Ardotalia) by Doctor's Gate, and with Temple-

borough. All the forts appear to have had earth ramparts surmounted by a wooden stockade with a single ditch or *vallum*.

With the building of Hadrian's Wall, Roman troops were withdrawn from the area, and the fort at Brough was dismantled, it being assumed that the Brigantes would be Roma-nised. However the Brigantes rose in revolt in AD 154-155. The revolt was suppressed, and a more permanent fort was rebuilt at Brough about AD

159. Further risings of the Brigantes took place in AD 197 and in the years that followed. To the north-west was the strategic fort at Melandra.

Apart from the military aspect of their occupation, the Romans had a commercial interest. Lead, which also contained silver, was important to the Roman economy, and it was obtained from various parts of Derbyshire, particularly around Wirksworth. Over thirty pigs of lead bearing Roman inscriptions have been found in Derbyshire, while other pigs bearing references to their Derbyshire origin have been located as far afield as Pulborough in Sussex, Falkirk, and near Brough in Yorkshire. It is probable that local inhabitants, who lived in caves or settlements like those at Cressbrook Dale and Robin Hood's Stride, worked the lead from mines which were imperial property. The pigs of lead were shipped either along the Trent to which they were carried by packhorse, or through the collecting centre of Navio and thence to the Roman port at Bawtry.

Although the lead itself was important the Romans were more interested in the silver content, but Derbyshire lead produced little silver. Pigs marked *EX ARG* indicate it was not bullion. References are made in Roman literature to the centre of the Derbyshire lead industry as being *Lutudarum*. The location of this place is not known, although it was most probably in the vicinity of Middleton-by-Wirksworth.

Romanised civilian settlement in the County was associated with villas (farm colonies) which were probably built on the lower-lying land of the south and east and have been excavated at Royston Grange in mid-Derbyshire. Sites of Roman pottery kilns have been excavated at Shottle, Hazelwood, Holbrook, Pleasley and at Derby where there was also an industrial settlement. On these sites coarse jars were manufactured to carry provisions, examples of which have been found as far north as Hadrian's Wall.

It has been suggested that the Romans worked Derbyshire 'Blue John', but the Roman source of this mineral is now known to have been in Northern Italy, and the earliest working of the semi-precious stone in Derbyshire dates from the eighteenth century. The Roman occupation, which ended in the early fifth century when Emperor Honorius told the British authorities 'to fend for themselves', made little impact on the landscape. The forts were either ignored or quarried by the later settlers, and only some sections of the road system remain with us today.

The withdrawal was part of a gradual pattern extending over the far-flung extremities of the Roman empire and left a well-administered but relatively defenceless country. Groups of westward-moving tribal groups in Eurasia was the reason the Saxons from north-west Germany came to the shores of Britain. During the last half of the fourth century, the Saxons came as plunderers sailing along the coasts and rivers, burning and pillaging. The Romano-British were unable to defend themselves, having depended upon the protec-

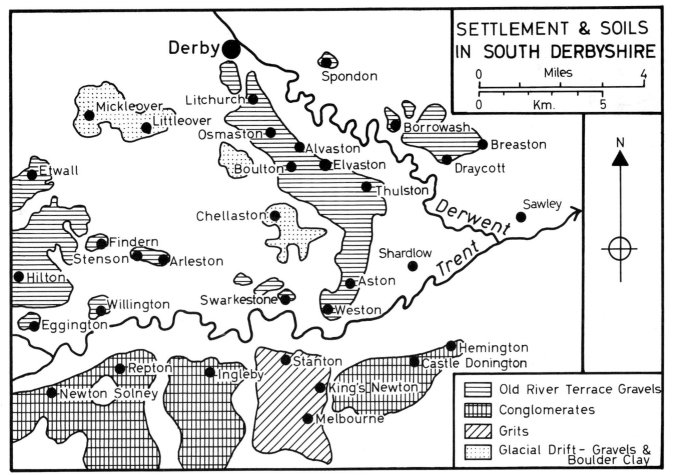

Settlements with Saxon place names and the soil/rock types in South Derbyshire.

Repton showing St Wystan's Church with the buildings of the school. In the foreground is the old course of the river used by the Saxons and later the Danes.

The Saxon crypt, Repton Church.

Bradbourne Cross, reassembled after being cut up for gate posts.

Eyam Cross, one of approximately thirty in the County. The upper two feet of the shaft is missing.

tion of Rome, nor do they appear to have traded, and eventually the plunderers became settlers.

The Saxons tended to avoid Roman settlements, and selected dry sites on the river terraces above the flood plain of a river, or in areas with a sandstone sub-soil, probably already occupied. Place-name evidence gives clues to the dominant culture existing in an area, but does not identify the earliest settlement. Their dependence upon domestic animals (*wic* from Latin *Vicus* indicates a dairy farm, village or settlement) meant that any rejuvenation of woodland was restricted, and in addition there was a need for hay. The place-name *field* suggests a clearing in woodland, whilst *ley* or *leah* is a clearing, but much woodland had disappeared in the Neolithic period. Some place-names suggest the use of fire to clear land as at Burnt Heath at Hilton, Burnsditch at Mickleover, or Burntwood at Dale. The extent of woodland at that time can be traced in the place-names which incorporate the names of trees like Ashbourne, Alderwasley, Elmton, Okeover and Hazelwood.

Under King Penda, the people of the Central Kingdom of Mercia ravaged Northumbria and destroyed St Aidan's settlement on the Farne Islands, an incident vividly described by the Venerable Bede. Bede also described how Christianity came to Repton after AD 653, and it was at Repton that the first religious house in Mercia was established, an abbey being established 'under the Saxon way' some time before AD 664. The crypt under the present church dates from AD 656, and was the burial site of King Wigston (Wystan) following his murder in AD 849. Miracles associated with his tomb resulted in Repton becoming a place of pilgrimage, with entrances to the crypt being rebuilt to accommodate the flow of pilgrims. Saxon stonework is also to be found in the churches at Bradbourne and Ault Hucknall, while crosses, as at Bakewell, Spondon, Bradbourne and Eyam, may date from this period, possibly erected before a church was built on the site. Derbyshire formed a section of the diocese of Mercia, and the County remained 'attached' to the See of

Lichfield until 1884 when the See of Southwell was founded. Among the many settlements associated with the Saxons was one at the confluence of the Markeaton and Bottle Brooks, which was named 'Northworthy', near the site of St Werburgh's Church in Derby and away from the Romano-British site. In mid-Derbyshire the Saxons, having established title to certain territory, settled where water was available in the limestone area. A series of suspended water-tables based on intrusive layers of impermeable volcanic rock probably account for the sites of Kniveton, Hognaston, Brassington, Parwich and Carsington, and this makes the 245-metre contour line of some significance.

The size of the settlements established by the Saxons varied markedly from one part of the County to another, a fact reflected in the present-day parish boundaries, many of which were based on the original Saxon boundaries between villages.

On the more fertile lower-lying land, the townships were smaller because a substantial population, probably dispersed, could be supported by a relatively small area of land. By contrast, the townships in upland areas, as for example Monyash, Ashover or Hartington, extended over much larger areas, much of which was waste that could only support sheep grazing, and often incorporating subsidiary settlements and scattered farms. The wide variation of soil type, climatic conditions and altitude, the proportion of land in arable, pasture, woodland and waste varied markedly from place to place, although in an era of self-sufficiency even the poorest villages had some arable land.

Such settlements operated on a communal basis under a lord who evolved a series of rights and privileges, inhabitants whether freeholders, villeins or serfs providing bodies for armed service and for work in the 'fields'. In the south and east

The site of Taddington, the highest village in Derbyshire, following the stream — Illy Willy Water. An example of an infield-outfield settlement, the infield near the village was the grain-growing land and enclosed (small, narrow fields) at an early date by agreement. The outfield — upland — was enclosed by Act of Parliament after 1795 and, because it is limestone, necessitated the creation of clay basins — meres — for water for animals.

of the County open-field villages of the traditional Midland pattern evolved. In the west and north, many villages never had a conventional open-field system, and in places such as Matlock and Glossop, arable farming, it would appear, was always carried out in small enclosed fields.

The origin of the so-called manorial system is obscure, but it is clear that the basic principles were evolved by the Saxons. This developed into the feudal system of tenure under the Normans and is the basis of the Domesday entries which dealt with estates, not individual settlements.

The division of the county into parishes, which were ecclesiastical units, came after the conversion of the Saxons to Christianity, possibly in the eighth century, and was linked to the upkeep of the church and its incumbent by contributions from the villagers — the tithe. In the densely populated lowlands, the parish often adopted the existing settlement boundaries, but in the sparsely populated areas, a single priest and church would serve an extensive area. Thus in the parish of Glossop there were the settlements of Hayfield, Mellor, Charlesworth, Chisworth, Chunal, Chinley, Ludworth, Simmondley, Whitfield, Dinting, Hadfield and Padfield.

The Anglo-Saxon kingdoms were constantly at war with each other as they struggled for dominance of land and resources. The burial site at Benty Grange, excavated by Thomas Bateman in the nineteenth century, and the Wigber Low site suggest such conflicts.

In AD 793, a fleet of long-boats appeared off Lindisfarne where the 'pirates' landed, robbed the church of its plate, killed the monks, and took the novices as slaves back to southern Scandinavia. This was one of many raids, and the marauders, whose raids extended as far as Bordeaux, became the scourge of the Anglo-Saxon coastal and estuarine dwellers. Gradually the Danish raiders settled in the coastal areas whence they pillaged inland, often raiding along the rivers. On one of these forays, the Danes, led by Ragnar Lodrok's sons, sailed up the Trent to Nottingham where they wintered in AD 867-8. Four years later, the same

band left their winter quarters at Torksey and wintered at Repton where they occupied the site of the abbey and scored a complete victory over the Mercians. Before this, the Saxons had removed the shrine of St Wystan to safety and it was not returned to Repton until AD 970. Later it was removed by Canute to Evesham Abbey. There is a similar story about St Alkmund. Alkmund, the son of the King of Northumbria, was killed by the Danes at Lilleshall in Shropshire. His sarcophagus was

taken by the Saxons to Northworthy where the site was later to become a place of pilgrimage.

It was during the last quarter of the ninth century that the Danes overran the area we now know as Derbyshire as a result of the campaigns of Halfdene and Guthrum. Place-names indicating settlements they took over, and upon which they imposed their culture, have the endings *-by* which meant a homestead, *-thorpe*, indicated an off-shoot settlement, and *-booth*, which was an

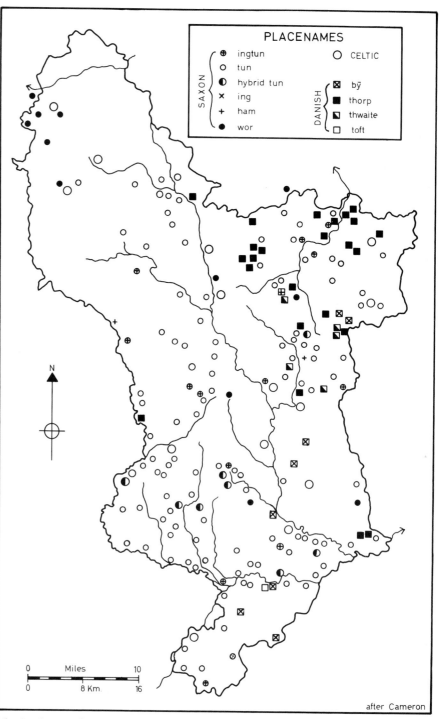

The distribution of place-name endings in the County: ('thwaite' indicates a Norse settlement).

Bakewell from the south-west, a nucleated settlement at a crossing point on the River Wye. A burgh (fortress) was built overlooking the site from its eastern side. The church has a stone cross and Saxon work in the porch. A collegiate church, it served a parish extending to Buxton, including Taddington. A market and fair charter dates from 1254 but had been 'held from time immemorial'. During the eighteenth century, the town's wells had to be deepened, suggesting a lowering of the water-table, the result of lead-mine drainage.

out-pasture. In some instances these settlements appear to occupy sites inferior in aspect and soil-type to those settled by the Saxons but this may reflect their agricultural practice. An aspect of Danish rule was the greater freedom of the individual compared with the restricted state of affairs under the Saxons. Under Danish occupation there was a class of men called Socmen. They, unlike the Saxon villeins and bordars, worked their own land separately from the communal activity of the village, although they were subservient to the lord of the manor.

Following the Treaty of Wedmore in AD 878, England was divided into the Kingdom of Wessex, and the Danelaw. South Derbyshire was near the frontier zone and as a result was fought over frequently. Derby was one of the five Danish Burghs, and it changed hands several times. Ethelfleda, Lady of the Mercians, captured the town from the Danes in AD 918, but at a heavy cost as a contemporary document describes: 'God helping her, before Lammas, got the town which is called Derby with all that belongs thereto, but there were also slain four of her thanes within the gates, which was a sorrow to her.' Tradition has it that Ethelfleda built the first bridge over the Derwent as a thanksgiving for the victory.

The Danish settlement at Derby was mentioned for the first time in AD 917, and was established on a site nearer the river Derwent, between the Saxon township of Northworthy and the Romano-British site. In AD 920, Edward the Elder, ruler of Wessex and brother of Ethelfleda 'fared into Peaceland to Badecanwyll (Bakewell) and bade work a burgh (fortress) there.' These fortresses were built to establish Wessex control of the land and by AD 942, King Edmund had freed the five burghs and the original Kingdom of Mercia 'as far as Dore and Whitwell Gap' from the Danes. Under the unifying kingship of Canute in 1013, Christianity and law and order once more prevailed over most of England, and in the eleventh century six churches were recorded in Derby; St Werburgh's, All Saints, St Michael's, St Alkmund's, St Mary's and St Peter's.

It is to the Danes that Derby owes its modern name, and also to them that Derbyshire traces its origins as a shire within the Danelaw, the first reference being in AD 1049. The shires were divided into smaller units called hundreds. In Derbyshire there were six hundreds — Appletree, Scarsdale, High Peak, Morleston and Litchurch, Repton and Gresley, and Wirksworth — which continued to be used as administrative units into the ninteenth century. The origin of the term *hundred,* like *parish,* is obscure but it is thought to have identified an area capable of supporting a hundred families or family groups. Under the Danes, these areas were called Wapentakes, only Wirksworth Wapentake retaining this title in the following centuries. The circular church site at Wirksworth suggests an earlier religious site and the ninth-century sarcophogus lid indicates its importance in Saxon Derbyshire.

The Battle of Hastings heralded the end of Saxon-Danish rule and the inception of Norman control. Following the Conquest, William allowed several of the Saxon lords to retain their lands under his overlordship, but most of the country was divided between his Norman knights, in return for their support. The King retained one-fifth of the land for himself, and allotted a quarter to the church, and he was careful to split the holdings of the lords so that no man was in a position to assemble a large rebel force. As a result of the re-apportionment of land there were vast changes in land-ownership and this was undoubtedly one of the reasons behind the immense undertaking of the Domesday Survey compiled in 1086.

The chief landowner in Derbyshire in 1086 was Henry de Ferrers, who held one hundred and fourteen manors. He also had a further ninety-six manors which were split up among thirteen other counties. De Ferrers' principal seat was at Duffield, where he built a castle reputedly second only in size to the Tower of London. The King held forty-four

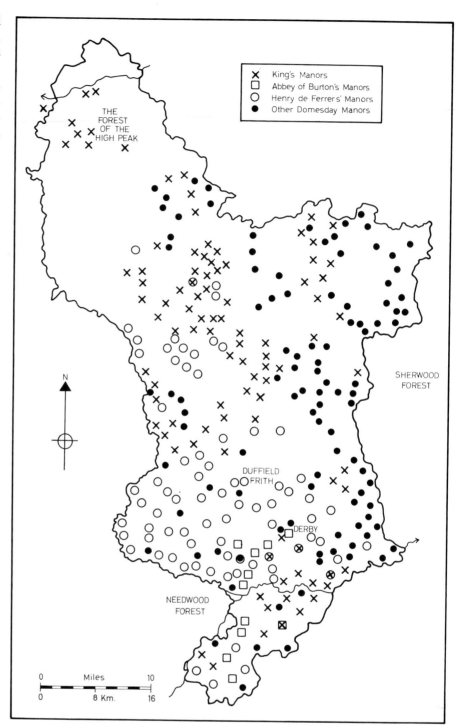

Distribution of land holdings at the time of Domesday.

manors in the County, which were distributed at intervals of approximately a day's march. Some of the manors, like Ashbourne, Parwich, Wirksworth, Metesford, Darley Abbey, Bakewell, Ashford and Hope, had been Royal manors during the reign of Edward the Confessor. Other knights who held manors in return for services to the King, assessed as knight's 'fiefs' or fees, were Ralph Fitzherbert with nineteen, William Peverel who held several manors in the north of the County where he

built castles at Bolsover and Castleton, the Abbot of Burton, the Earl of Chester and Geoffrey de Aslin. These lords provided their military vassals with estates carved out of their own lands and were given in exchange an undertaking to supply the lord with the services of a fully-armed knight and his necessary servants for up to forty days each year. Eventually, payment was made by rent, and the knights' fees were often divided among several tenants.

The manorial economy of the

Castleton, where on Oak Apple Day (29 May) the Garland King on horseback leads a procession to the church where a garland is hoisted on to one of the pinnacles of the tower. The origin of the custom is a mystery.

The manor of Bolsover was held in 1086 by Robert for his overlord, William Peverel. The first castle was of timber surrounded by a deep ditch. It was William's son who built a stone castle. William Peverel's grandson forfeited the castle and his estates to the Crown in 1155. The present structure was built for Bess of Hardwick by Robert Smythson. It was about this time that the grid-patterned town with a central axis was laid out. The market area has been reduced by building encroachment. The market was confirmed by a charter of 1225/6.

southern portion of Derbyshire resembled that of the rest of Midland England. The lord of the manor usually held about one-half of his land in demesne, which he farmed directly, usually under the control of his bailiff. This was cultivated by his villeins who, along with their families, were the property of the lord to be sold or given away as he pleased as at Breadsall in the thirteenth century, and at Wensley in 1324.

The freemen of the manor held lands for which they paid farms, which were fixed rents and services, to the lord to whom they were bound by 'fealty', that is a sacred oath to be his vassal. The number of freemen in Derbyshire, although none are enumerated as such in Domesday, appears to have been large and derived from the Danish period.

In the upland area an infield-outfield cultivation would appear to have operated, with early piecemeal enclosure of the infield, rents replacing service to the Lord.

The decision to undertake the Domesday Survey was taken at a full meeting of the *curia regis* held at Gloucester during Christmas 1085. The following year the Royal Commissioners visited each shire when, at a special meeting of the shire court, the landowners were questioned, and their answers given under oath. The answers were written down in Latin by clerks on rolls of parchment, and were checked by the questioning of sworn juries of villagers which consisted of the village priest, the reeve and six of the inhabitants. Townsmen as well as villagers were questioned.

Inevitably in such a vast undertaking, the Survey was only part completed, and the returns were not properly arranged. Also the death of the King in 1087 cut short its completion. The result of the survey was the Domesday Book, which was a summary of the findings, and naturally such data has to be treated with circumspection. In the case of the Abbot of Burton, the return to the Commissioners was only a summary and does not reveal the true nature of the Abbey's holdings.

Domesday Book's Derbyshire entries reveal extensive tracts of uncultivated land, a third of it classed

Peak Castle, built by William Peverel, Sheriff of Nottinghamshire and Derbyshire, bailiff of the Royal Manors of north Derbyshire. The present keep was erected by Henry II in 1176 after Peverel lost his estates (1155). It was the seat of the Keeper of the Royal Forest of the High Peak, and a hunting lodge. Henry I and Henry II extended the area of the forest which was mainly unwooded upland.

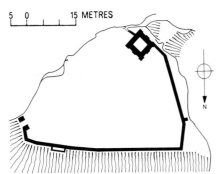

as woodland and a tenth as waste or unused land, including upland, marsh and fen. These areas were designated by William the Conqueror as 'royal forest', the one in the County being the Forest of the High Peak. Some of the waste may have been attributable to the scorched-earth policy to which William resorted in putting down risings. In the Mercian revolt of 1069, forty-three vills or townships were totally destroyed and twenty-five partially so, though these were not all in Derbyshire.

Although the basic pattern of settlement was as widespread as it is today, the extensive area of nineteenth-century development on the coalfield was, at the time of Domesday, predominantly waste and woodland. Some settlements referred to in 1086 have disappeared, while others like Buxton are not mentioned, probably because it was included in a larger area. In general, the distribution of settlement reflects the agricultural potential of the County, but lead-mining accounts for the importance of Wirksworth, and possibly Ashford, Crich and Matlock Bridge. Most settlements were recorded as having a church or a shared one, as at Brailsford, and also a watermill. A feature in Derbyshire was the berewick, which was a subsidiary or out-lying estate of the main manor.

Domesday Derby, although a larger area than today, showed a decline in population: there were one hundred burgesses in 1086, where there had been 243 at the time of King Edward, and 103 houses were waste, perhaps a result of the earthquake of 1048, and suggests that the town suffered at the hands of William in

Below Peak Castle is Peak Cavern, which in the nineteenth century had cottages inside the cave entrance, and a rope walk.

1069. The burgesses held rights to the extensive fields outside the 'borough' at Cornum (Quarndon) and Detton (Little Eaton). They paid their taxes to the King, and were outside the jurisdiction of the Lords of the Manors. It was the burgesses who sought to consolidate their privileges and gain new ones by applying for a succession of Royal Charters.

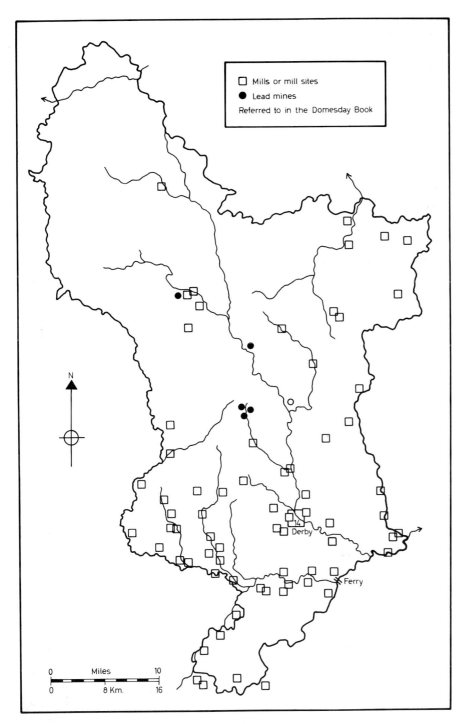

Mills or mill sites
Lead mines
Referred to in the Domesday Book

N

Miles
0   10
0   8 Km.   16

Derby

Ferry

The other taxes for the County were paid to the Sheriff, an official created before the Conquest. He was chosen by the King, and responsible to him alone for the administration of local finance, the execution of justice and the maintenance of the customs whereby the shire was governed.

The County Sheriff was first identified in the reign of Etheldred II and by the end of the Confessor's reign he was the King's chief executive agent in every branch of local government, replacing the position of the earl. For administrative purposes, the Counties of Derby and Nottingham were linked until 1566 when an Act was passed giving a separate Sheriff to each. In the list of Sheriffs for the joint counties from 1131, the names of Cokayne, Babington, Curzon, Eyre, Franceys, Fitzherbert, Foljambe, Kniveton, Gresley, Grey, Leach, Leeke, Longford, Meynell, Okeover, Pole, Strelley and Vernon appear most regularly. Between 1425 and 1450, nineteen of the Sheriffs were Derbyshire men of military repute, but previously Nottinghamshire knights predominated. The preeminence of Nottingham is clear in the Domesday Book, Derby being listed under the entry for that place.

Masters and Men

AFTER the establishment of Norman rule churches and monasteries were built which reflected the importance of the Church, and castles and manor houses were constructed which emphasised the overlordship of the nobility. It was also a period which saw the development of boroughs, in particular the important market centres of Derby and Chesterfield, and also the establishment of a pattern of land tenure which in places was to last into the early nineteenth century.

The forty-eight churches recorded in the Domesday Survey by no means indicate all those that existed then, Chesterfield being an obvious omission. The County was in the See of Lichfield, but between the twelfth and ninteenth centuries, much of the Peak was exempt from the Bishop of Lichfield's episcopal jurisdiction, being part of what was termed the 'peculiar jurisdiction of the Dean and Chapter of Lichfield' (the Dean and Chapter being responsible for the fabric of the Cathedral and needing their own estates to produce revenue for this purpose).

This did not mean that the extensive parishes of Bakewell, Hope and Tideswell were neglected; indeed there were frequent visitations to the area, when the chief business was the presenting of offenders for sins of incontinence, drunkenness and slander, as well as for ecclesiastical irregularities, and the proving of wills. Most of the rest of Derbyshire came into the bishop's jurisdiction but there were other smaller areas of peculiar jurisdiction such as Dale Abbey and Peak Forest. He was not only dean of the collegiate church of All Saints in Derby, but also held rectorial tithes and the appointment to the vicarages of the major churches at Chesterfield, Wirksworth and Ashbourne, as well as the patronage of others. In the south of the County, the See of Carlisle had the endowment of the church at Melbourne, and it was there that the Bishops of Carlisle had a palace to which they retreated when forced to by the incursions of the Scots. Similarly the Bishops of Chester had connections with Sawley.

The south door of St Michael's Church, Melbourne, with the possible chantry of St Catherine's — licensed in 1380 — to the rear abutting on the barn-like building which was a malting in the eighteenth century.

Chesterfield Church. Mostly erected in the first half of the fourteenth century, it was restored by Gilbert Scott in 1843. The oldest part of the church structure is the thirteenth-century supports of the crossing tower. The twisted spire is accounted for by the delay in adding the lead 'tiles', so allowing the timbers to warp. The wealth of the guilds at the time is reflected in the four chapels at the east end, the earliest founded in 1218.

A large number of parish churches were in the hands of monasteries in the twelfth century, and these parishes were practically withdrawn from episcopal control, particularly where the living was a good one. In 1205 the church at Bradbourne, with its four large chapelries, was given to the Priory of Dunstable. The priory did not appropriate the church until 1278, when several canons of Dunstable were sent to reside at Bradbourne under the title of wardens. These wardens accounted to the prior for the profits which were accumulated from the payment of tithes. In the same way the canons of Darley Abbey held episcopal jurisdiction over the parishioners of the churches of St Peter, St Michael and St Werburgh in Derby, and those of Crich, Pentrich, Ashover and South Wingfield. The abbot therefore held the lion's share of the emoluments. Annual proceeds were paid by Derbyshire churches to the various abbeys and priories in and around the County, and elsewhere.

The income of the clergy could be large, as was the case with the vicar of Ashbourne who, it was agreed by the Deanery of Lincoln in 1290, should receive all mortuaries; that is, at the death of the householder or the householder's wife, the second best beast was taken by the vicar (save

horses), tithes of flax and hemp, tithes of pigs, geese, fruit, gardens, colts and calves, Lent dues and offerings whether in money or kind, tithes of mills of the whole parish, tithes of corn and hay at Great and Little Clifton, tithes of hay at Methley, Longdolles and Earls Meadow, and half tithes of corn at Methley. He was also provided with a Vicarage house.

Derbyshire had comparatively few religious houses within its borders, and out of the fifty-six rectories that were eventually appropriated, the tithes of only twenty-two remained in the County; nine to Darley Abbey, four to Dale Abbey, three each to Beauchief Abbey and Repton Priory, two to Gresley Priory and one to King's Mead. Breadsall Priory received the rectorial tithes of half a

church at Mugginton. It is clear therefore that the church was important in the temporal affairs of the parish, as it was also a wealthy institution through material goods acquired as a result of the tithes and other emoluments. Its status at the time is exemplified by the fine churches that were built.

At the time of the Conquest there was not a single monastic house in Derbyshire, though Burton Abbey, just over the Staffordshire border, which had been established by the Benedictine order in 1004, owned lands in South Derbyshire, and in the years following the Conquest was granted the Royal Manor of Mickleover with its berewicks of Findern, Potlock and Littleover. In the two centuries following the Conquest, a

Remains of Beauchief Abbey, a Premonstatentian monastery founded c.1176 by Robert Fitzranulph, allegedly an assassin of Thomas à Becket. The engraving, by Sir Francis Chantrey, originally appeared in Ebenezer Rhodes' Peak Scenery *(1817-1823) and in John Croston's* Chantrey's Peak Scenery *(1889).*

number of religious houses were established. The Augustine canons set up houses at Calke and Church Gresley and a small oratory, dedicated to St Helen, in Derby in the first half of the twelfth century.

A large abbey, dedicated to St Mary, was built at Darley on the northern outskirts of Derby in the mid-twelfth century. A result of gifts from patrons such as Robert de Ferrers and Hugh, Dean of Derby, along with the purchase of land, the Abbey at Darley became a large landowner. At the time of the Dissolution in 1535, when inventories were made of their plate

and removable goods, the Abbey had an annual value of £258 13s 5d (£258.66) which included the great tithes of Bolsover, Crich, Mackworth, Pentrich, South Wingfield, Scarcliffe and Palterton, and St Michael's in Derby, as well as the tithes of lamb and wool from Bolsover, Scarcliffe and South Wingfield, plus the pensions from the churches at Brailsford and Uttoxeter.

An unsuccessful attempt had been made by the Augustine canons to establish a house at Dale, but in the 1150s, they were granted by the Countess of Chester, 'in free and

perpetual gift the working of the quarry of Rependene (Repton) by the Trent, together with the advowson of the Church of St Wystan of Rependene with all things pertaining thereto on the condition that when a fitting opportunity shall occur, a convent shall be established there as a mother house.' The opportunity occurred in 1172, when the canons deserted Calke and moved to Repton Priory with its own church, built on a site close to the site of the Saxon abbey. In the thirteenth century, the same canons established a small priory at Breadsall. The two other large monastic houses to be established in the County were at Dale, about 1160, and at Beauchief between 1172 and 1186, the canons being of the Premonstratensian order.

The Nunnery of St Mary-de-Pratis was set up in Derby, on the banks of the Markeaton Brook, by the Abbot of Darley in 1160. Like many small religious institutions, it was always in financial difficulties. Also in Derby the Cluniac monks had a small house dedicated to St James which was attached to Lenton Abbey, near Nottingham, and it was this house which established the seventeen-day great fair of St James. Other small houses included one at Temple Normanton, under the aegis of the Knights Hospitallers of St John of Jerusalem, and the leper hospitals at Locko, in Derby, and possibly at Alkmonton and Chesterfield (Old Spital). The Black Friars, who came to England in the thirteenth century, established a Friary in Derby in what is today's Friar Gate.

The larger Derbyshire religious houses had a considerable number of farms or granges scattered throughout the County. Examples of these can be seen in the large, isolated farmhouses of today which have the names Griff Grange, Monyash Grange, Mouldridge Grange, Benty Grange, Bostern Grange, Roystone Grange and One Ash Grange. In the main the granges were run by the monks as extensive sheep runs, wool forming the most important saleable product of the monasteries, several of which mortgaged their wool production for some years ahead, to carry out large building programmes.

Darley Abbey had Normanton

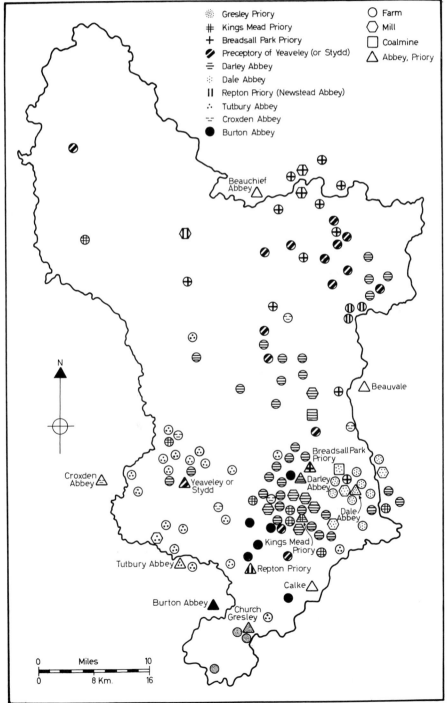

Religious Houses holding lands in Derbyshire at the time of the Dissolution

Buildwas Abbey (Staffs)	—	Wenbroke Grange
Trentham (Staffs)	—	Sutton Rectory, Ilkeston, Bradbourne
Rocester (Staffs)	—	Hognaston, Kynston, Scropton, Edensor
Garendon (Leics)	—	Hartington, Bradbourne
Langley Priory (Leics)	—	Charleston, Boulton
Grace Dieu Priory (Leics)	—	Dalbury Lees, Staley, Woodthorp, Bradley
Preceptory of Hether (Leics)	—	Rawston
Croxton (Leics)	—	Dale, Wyggeley, Chesterfield
St Mary Pratis (Leics)	—	Youlgreave, Stanton, Winster, Haddon, Measham, Chaddesden, Middleton Moor
Laund	—	Hathersage, Chapel-en-le-Frith
Breedon Priory	—	The Peak
Louth Park Abbey (Lincs)	—	Burley Grange
Semprinham Priory	—	Walton
Vale Royal Monastery (Cheshire)	—	Castleton
Abbey of West Chester	—	Weston, Aston, Morley, Wilne, Shardlow, Smalley, Derby
Bisham Abbey (Berks)	—	Mollesden (Derby)
Dunstable Priory	—	Bradbourne
Shelford Priory (Notts)	—	Ockbrook
Rufford	—	Chesterfield, Brampton
Lenton Abbey	—	Ashford, Chelmorton, Monyash, Chapel, Horsley, Denby, Chesterfield, Brampton, Whitwell, Tideswell old mill, Bakewell mill
Welbeck Abbey	—	Etwall, Duckmanton, North Wingfield, Wingerworth, Newbold
Thurgarton Priory	—	Pilsley, Boylestone
Beauvale	—	Etwall
Worksop Priory	—	Shirebrook, Whitwell
Monasteries of the Minorities without Aldgate (London)	—	Hartington
Bermondsey Monastery (London)	—	St James, Derby
Kenilworth	—	Cronxton, Pilsbury
Great Malvern	—	Marsham
Roche (Yorks)	—	Grange in the Peak. One Ash
Monk Bretton	—	Beighton
Doncaster (Grey Friars)	—	Beighton

Grange which was assessed at the Dissolution as having '18 oxen, ten kyne, seven horses and a large number of pigs.' This stock, along with fifty loads of hay, several wains and carts and a smith's forge was sold for £168 13s 4d (£168.66). Some of the religious houses were also involved in the early development of local industries, particularly the exploitation of coal. The Abbeys of Dale, Burton, and Beauvale in Nottinghamshire, leased the rights to mine coal on their land. Dale Abbey had a cornmill on the Derwent at Borrowash, and Darley Abbey made a sluice with nine floodgates on the same river at Breadsall in the 1270s.

The Derbyshire monastic houses appear to have been reasonably well conducted, though it was not always so. In the fifteenth century, Bishop Redman, on a visit to Dale, found the canons keeping dogs and puppies, gambling, performing divine service without due reverence, eating in secular houses and ignoring the rule of silence. This bad discipline he blamed on the 'imbecility and impotence' of the aged Abbot, who was retired on a pension.

Following the Dissolution of the Monasteries, much of the monastic property was sold by the Sovereign to members of the gentry. Except at Repton, where the 'nest was destroyed lest the birds should build again', the son of Thomas Thacker of Heage

being responsible for the demolition of the priory church and buildings in the 1550s (supposedly in one day!), the monastic buildings were not immediately destroyed, but in the course of time they became quarries for the building of yeomen homes and the growing number of small country houses. The Friary in Derby became the town house of John Sharpe, gentleman.

The authority of the knights in the period after the Conquest is reflected in the castles that were built. Following the building of Duffield Castle, the de Ferrers were given constable rights by King John, but this was short-lived as the castle was despoiled following Robert de Ferrers' part in the rising against Henry III in 1266. Across the Derwent valley from Duffield was Horston Castle, built some time in the mid-twelfth century by the de Buron family, who were Lords of the Manor of Horsley. Presumably it was built to protect an important river crossing on the route between Wirksworth and Nottingham. In 1204, Horston Castle became a Royal stronghold, passing in an exchange of estates to King John, who proceeded to strengthen it and to improve its amenities. Codnor Castle, built by Henry de Grey in the thirteenth century, passed to the Zouch family late in the fifteenth century. When the estates passed as part-payment for indebtedness to the Willoughbys in 1634, the castle was already in a state of disrepair.

Other castles were built at Melbourne, where the Duke of Bourbon was imprisoned following his capture at Agincourt, at Bretby, Castle Gresley, Mackworth and Repton. The motte and bailey castle at Repton was important in the civil war between King Stephen and Matilda in the 1140s. In the north of the County, William Peverel built castles at Bolsover and Castleton.

The Norman castle at Bolsover was already in ruin when Bess of Hardwick's second son, Sir Charles Cavendish, bought it in 1613 and began to rebuild it as his residence. William Peverel, bailiff of the Royal manors in the north of Derbyshire, built Peak Castle overlooking the village of Castleton which was then enlarged

Smerrill Grange showing deserted house plots. Desertion may have occured after the Dissolution when Abbey support ceased.

The remains of Dale Abbey. Several buildings in the village incorporate parts of the abbey buildings.

to service it. The small defensive keep was built by Henry II in 1176 at a cost of £180, some twenty years after the castle had passed into Royal hands, following the confiscation of the Peverel estates because William had supported the upstart Stephen. In 1157, Henry II received the submission of Malcolm, King of Scotland, at the castle, the occasion being celebrated with wine to the value of seventy-two shillings.

The original purpose of Peak Castle was to control the wild area of the Peak, much of which was taken up by the Forest of the High Peak. This was an area of bleak moorland with patches of ash woodland and was used by the kings for hunting. However, within the Forest area were pockets of cultivated 'infield' reclaimed from the moorland, while on its edges were settlements such as Glossop, Chapel-en-le-Frith and Tideswell.

Bordering the County were Sherwood and Needwood Forests, but these, like Duffield Frith (or Forest), were later creations. Duffield Frith did not become a Royal forest in law until 1399, but it had been a hunting area since the time of the de Ferrers. In 1266, it passed into the hands of the Duchy of Lancaster, becoming

The arch of the chancel east window of Dale Abbey with the present church of All Saints' standing in front of the sandstone cliff in which there is a hermitage cave. The box-pewed church with the late-13th-century paintings was a 'Peculiar'. It is attached to a house, at one time a farm, post-office or inn. The church register has an entry: '1692, Dec 4. One couple married. Names unknown.'

part of the Honour (the holdings of a tenant-in-chief) of Tutbury, which was administered from the Lord's seat at Tutbury Castle. In 1313/14, Tutbury Priory received twenty deer as title from Duffield Frith. Duffield Frith was surrounded by palings, which tenants of land abutting upon the forest perimeter had to keep in repair. In this respect it differed from the High Peak Forest, the boundaries of which were natural features like 'the river Goyt as far as the Etherow',

or boundary stones or crosses. Within the Duffield Frith were several parks, each surrounded by pales. The most important of these was Ravensdale Park, to the west of Mugginton, where there was a Royal hunting lodge. This had a chapel, for which painted glass costing sixteen shillings was bought in 1313, where Edward I, Edward II and Henry IV stayed. Other parks can be identified in the present landscape by the names of isolated farms such as Holland

Park, Mansell Park, Wild Park and Park Farm. Duffield Frith was divided into four wards: Hulland, Belper, Duffield and Colebrook, for each of which a forester was in charge. A tombstone in Wirksworth Church bears the forester's emblem of office — a bugle and sword. The chapel for the Duffield Frith was at Belper and was first mentioned in 1272/3. Forest law differed from one forest to another, but forest justice was dispensed at the Justice Seat

The linear settlement of Tideswell which became an important market for wool (like Chapel-en-le-Frith) with a fourteenth-century church, former grammar school buildings, all reflecting its medieval prosperity. Byng (Lord Torrington) in 1790 stayed at the 1730 George Inn.

which, in the case of the High Peak, was at Castleton, Tideswell and Bowden where there was also a forestry residence or hall to which a chapel was attached. The chief administrator of the Peak was called the bailiff, whose responsibility it was to render annual accounts to the Crown or Duchy.

The verderers, whose symbol was an axe, were other forest officers directly responsible to the Crown, and were elected by the freeholders in the County court. There were four of these for the Peak, and their chief function was to preserve the vert (timber rights) and vension. If the foresters found a man trespassing on the vert, they would arrest him and

bail him to appear at the next forest court. However, if a man was caught killing or taking away a deer he was imprisoned until delivered on bail by the King or the justice of the particular forest. To look after the various possible abuses of the forest, a hierarchy of officers was created including the woodward, the agister and the ranger. In Duffield Frith, a duty was to see that the Parks were cleared of other stock in time of snow and hard weather to preserve grazing for deer. A 'deer house' was built in Belper Ward in 1313/14. In the early fifteenth century, the officers were required to make an annual census of deer (in March).

Every three years a survey was made

of the timber in the forest. In 1560 there were 12,000 oaks in Duffield Frith, and half as many twenty-seven years later. By the Civil War, much of Duffield Frith had been cleared, and Shottle and Postern Parks, and Colebrook Ward had been privately enclosed. The inhabitants of Duffield Ward, however, retained common rights until the late eighteenth century. The problem of rabbit warrens was dealt with in the seventeenth century: 'moulds and ffences' of a warren in the Holland Ward of the Forest of Duffield 'were thrown down, and the said . . .parte layed comon as fformerly by the Inhabitants of ye said Fforest.' In 1650, the forest was exploited for its coal, £30

Somersal Herbert Hall, built in 1564 for John Fitzherbert at a time before a restriction was placed on the use of timber (oak) for building.

being due for ' . . .the mines delfes or pitts of coale now in use or hearafter to be digged . . .and of erecting cottages for the habitacion of collyers with free passage for horses, carts and carriage passing to and from the said coal delfes.'

The transition from castle to manor house is well illustrated in Wingfield Manor. Lord Cromwell commenced the building of the Manor in 1441 but died before it was completed; it was finished by John Talbot, second Earl of Shrewsbury. In the ensuing years it saw the imprisonment of Mary Queen of Scots, and was a centre of Royalist resistance during the Civil War. After 1666 it came into the possession of Immanuel Hatton, a close friend of John Flamstead of Little Hallam, near Ilkeston, who was the first Astronomer Royal.

Haddon Hall, another manor house, was built in the twelfth century by the Avenels, passing by marriage to the Vernons in 1170.

Various manor house sites can be identified in the homestead mounds and the moated sites throughout the County.

Throughout the mediaeval period the economy was one of local self-sufficiency in much the same way that administration and justice were also locally promulgated. Justice was meted out by the local plenipotentiary at the Baron Court, while the administration of the manor was operated through the Court Leet.

The sole representative of Royal justice and administration was the Sheriff, who was supported by the occasional visits of the Justices in their progress to the Assize Courts. Because the Sheriff was the sole representative of Royal justice, and therefore much of the law and order was dealt with by the lords of the manor in their own way, Parliament in 1341 created the Justices of the Peace, bringing the local gentry into the adminstration of Royal justice

and by doing so, curbed the power of sheriffs and the manor courts.

Feuds between local families was an aspect of life as each attempted to upstage the other. In the Ashbourne area in the fourteenth and fifteenth centuries, the Cockayne family frequently feuded with their neighbours, including the Blounts and the Longfords. This feuding reached its culmination in the Civil War, when many local scores were settled.

The self-sufficient economy was based on the open-field system of agriculture and on feudal tenure, but the pattern differed from north to south and from west to east in response to the nature of the soil and the extent of woodland. In the north and west the economy was based in the main on livestock, chiefly sheep and cattle, with oats grown on the 'infield', but where the soil was more productive, a field system was operated. In certain areas the agricultural economy of the village and manor

Wingfield Manor, partly dismantled in 1646 and quarried by Immanuel Halton's grandson in 1774 to build Wingfield Hall.

was supplemented by a home-based woollen textile industry and by lead-mining, and in the neighbourhood of towns the weekly markets stimulated a more than self-sufficient economy.

Overall, the cultivated area of the County was small compared with the total. It is doubtful if Derbyshire ever produced sufficient grain to feed its populace, although Sir Anthony Fitzherbert, who lived at Norbury, in his *Boke of Husbandry* (1523) reported that 'usually rye and wheat mixture are grown, but also oats . . .' Grain was in fact imported from the Netherlands, by way of Hull and the River Trent. That areas of the County traded with each other is shown by the number of market charters granted in the thirteenth century, including Chesterfield (1204), Heanor (1243), Tideswell (1251), Alfreton (1252), Ilkeston (1252), Sandiacre (1252), Bakewell (1254), Ashbourne (1257), and Glossop (1290). Other centres such as

Cubley (1251), Aston-on-Trent (1257), Sawley (1259) and Mapperley (1267) received charters to hold fairs, these tending to specialise in a particular commodity.

Famine was fairly common in the Middle Ages, often resulting in a rise in the price of grain, as, for example, in 1294, when the price of corn rose to twenty-one shillings a quarter in the area of the Peak, this being about four times the average. The Black Death, which reached Derbyshire in May 1349, appears to have affected most settlements in the County including Derby, Eckington, Langwith, Mugginton, Bolsover, Longford, Willington, Pentrich as well as the priories of Beauchief, Dale and Gresley There is reference in 1365 to a shortage of chaplains in the years following the plague.

Recurrence of the plague in 1362 resulted in eleven tenants at Walton-on-Trent dying in bondage. These eleven tenants accounted for nearly three-quarters of the rents of the

village. As a result new tenants, when they could be found, paid the same rent but no longer gave service, thus being free of 'bondage'. At Palterton, no tenant survived and the land remained uncultivated for twenty-five years. As a result of this, large acreages were either returned to permanent fallow, which resulted in a less productive area of arable, and fewer families — a downward spiral — or they reverted to commonland, the lord of the manor using the extra grazing for his own benefit. This was a period of depopulation in both the upland Peak where cultivation was near its climatic and economic limit, and also in the lowlands, where whole villages disappeared.

Tenants in the hundred years following the Black Death were able to obtain long leases at low rents, or demand excessive wages, as in the Hundred of Morleston and Litchurch, where one hundred and twenty people were summoned under the Statute of Labourers. This state

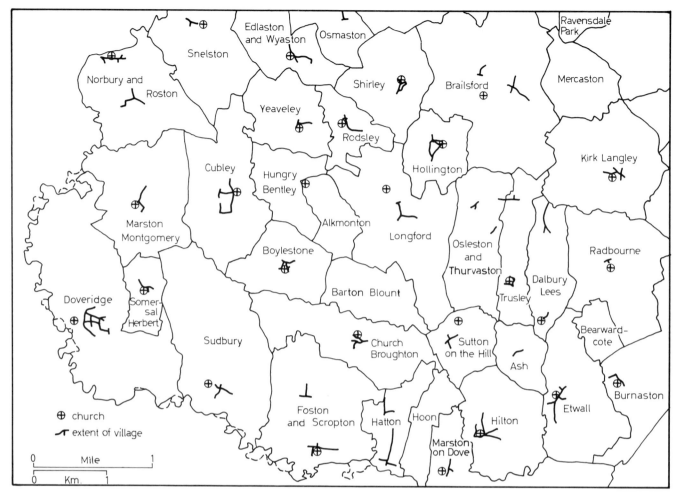

The parishes to the west of Derby, showing the extent of the villages and churches. No church could indicate a 'deserted site'. At Cubley, the community moved from the low-lying site near the church to a drier position. Further north, Birchover moved from an exposed site to the present more sheltered position.

of affairs aided by inflation, enabled peasants to become landlords, as was the case with the Holdens of Aston-on-Trent. Other families, like the Beresfords, sent their sons to London, leaving the lands to be managed by bailiffs. In this way many of the smaller estate-owning families originated.

Barton Blount, one of thirty-three deserted village sites recorded in the County (1968), has the sites of many timber buildings which ceased to exist after the fifteenth century.

Royal Tidings

BY THE early sixteenth century, the losses of population, experienced as a result of the Black Death and successive plagues, had been made up, and the economy of the County had become more stable, with arable land brought back into cultivation. Kinder, in 1663, referred to the district around Aston-on-Trent and Elvaston as 'the granary of Derbyshire', and another commentator wrote: 'Scarsdale be among as gallant corne counties as be in England.' Grain production in the south and east of the County must have been high to sustain the beer production of Burton upon Trent and Derby.

However, the north and west of the County continued to concentrate on sheep and cattle. Norden in 1607 described the grazing grounds on the banks of the Dove as among the best in England, while Fitzherbert considered sheep the most profitable livestock, the ewes' milk being made into cheese. Derbyshire cattle were described as 'of stately shape, bigge round and well-bucked in every manner, short-jointed and most comely to the eye, so that they are esteemed excellent in the market'. Labourers were paid between fourteen and twenty shillings (70p to £1) a year, while thatchers and sheep shearers received five pence (2p) a day. In 1634 a shepherd received 23s 4d (£1.17p) a year.

The weakening of feudal tenure in the fourteenth century resulted in a gradual consolidation of strip-holdings in the open fields. A survey at Ashford in 1608 shows tenants exchanging their arable strips in order to consolidate their holdings,

The Bretby Heifer bred by the Earl of Chesterfield.

and in the High Peak the enclosure of any area of less than five acres was not considered prejudicial to anyone. However, earlier in 1493 at Matlock, the King's tenants complained to the High Steward of the Honour of Tutbury that 'they ben gretly wronged by Philip Leche esquier that where they and other the Kinges tenauntes there have comyn for their catell without interpucion of any man . . .and now the said Philip hath closed in the said comyn XI acres and more to the gret hurte et enpoverish-ing of the said tenauntes'. Philip Leche was the owner of Chatsworth at this time. Between 1500 and 1650, enclosures of the common land took place at Belper, Duffield, Scropton, Alderwasley, Bowden, Spondon. Mellor, Parwich, Buxton, Fairfield, Tunstead, Bonsall, Priestcliff, Wirksworth, and at Chinley where there was opposition.

Although the County's population had returned to 50,000 — the level prior to the Black Death — there was little further growth owing to frequent outbreaks of plague and cholera. In 1586/7, the 'sweating sickness' killed every man in St Peter's Parish in Derby, and in the same year 355 burials at Chesterfield were recorded. The most disastrous outbreak was that of 1665 when six-sevenths of the population of Eyam died, possibly due to the misguided efforts of parson Mompesson to totally isolate his flock. The headless cross, which stands in Friar Gate, is a reminder of the plague in Derby. Goods were placed for sale, and money left in payment, on the cross.

During the sixteenth century, the County was never able to raise more than nine hundred men to fight for the King. Dury in *The East Midlands and the Peak* states: 'the return of

The plague cottage at Eyam where George Vicars, a journeyman tailor, received a box of clothes from London in September 1665.
His death four days later was associated with the plague germ carried with the clothes.

able-bodied men in Derbyshire in 1635, showed 65 per cent of the County total in the semi-industrial districts of Wirksworth, the High Peak, and Scarsdale, that is, in the areas of leadmines, coalmines, stone-pits, ironstone quarries and iron-works.'

An important family came to Derbyshire in the sixteenth century — that of the Cavendishes of Suffolk, where they held large estates. It was William Cavendish who was appointed a commissioner, under Thomas Cromwell, to visit and take surrender of various monastic houses at the Dissolution, for which he was rewarded with a knighthood and gifts of monastic lands. William Cavendish married the twenty-seven-year-old widow Elizabeth Hardwick, the daughter of an obscure Derbyshire squire, John Hardwick. Elizabeth's first marriage, at the age of twelve, had ended almost immediately in widowhood following the death of her ailing, fourteen-year-old husband, Robert Barlow. As a result of his death, Elizabeth acquired land at

Oldcotes and Hardwick which was to form the basis of her future wealth.

William Cavendish was persuaded by Bess to sell his Suffolk estates and to purchase the Chatsworth estate from her sister's husband, Francis Leche, in 1553. Together, they began to build the first Chatsworth House, of which there is little trace today, but before it was completed, Sir William died. Bess was left with six children, and the supervision of 375 workmen, who were completing the house. As a wealthy widow she had little difficulty in ensnaring Sir William St Loe, who was Captain of Queen Elizabeth's Guard and Grand Butler of England. Again the marriage was a short one, ending with the death of St Loe in 1565.

Three years later, she married her fourth husband, George Talbot, sixth Earl of Shrewsbury, Lord Lieutenant of Yorkshire, Nottinghamshire and Derbyshire, High Steward of England, Knight of the Garter, wealthy and influential widower, 'whom she brought to Terms of the greatest Honour and Advantage to herself and

children.' This she achieved by the inter-marriage of their respective sons and daughters.

The couple had no housing problem, the Earl owning or having responsibility for Sheffield Castle, Sheffield Manor, Wingfield Manor, Tutbury Castle, Worksop Manor, Buxton Hall and Rufford Abbey, while Bess had Chatsworth. In the course of their marriage, they acquired Bolsover and Welbeck Abbey. For the reconstruction and refurbishing of her houses, Bess employed the services of the Smyth-sons of Bolsover who were mason-architects, and she exploited to the full the products of her estates: alabaster at fourteen shillings a ton from Tutbury, black marble from Ashford, timber from Heath and Stainsby, lime from Skegby and Crich, and lead from Barlow.

The numerous houses turned out to be a doubtful blessing. When looking for a custodian for Mary Queen of Scots, Queen Elizabeth saw the Earl of Shrewsbury as an ideal candidate. During her fifteen years in

The original Chatsworth House was built in 1557. The fourth Earl of Devonshire was responsible for replacing this, following his father's death in 1684, the new house being designed by William Talman. The sixth Duke of Devonshire modified and extended it in the early nineteenth century, using the architect Sir James Wyatville. James Paine designed the stables in the later half of the eighteenth century.

the Earl's charge, Mary wandered unhappily from house to house, sometimes living in comfort, at other times in grim austerity. At Tutbury Castle where she complained of the smell, Mary was permitted a retinue of two secretaries, five gentlemen-in-waiting, fourteen servants, three cooks, four pages, three valets, a doctor, a surgeon, an apothecary and

an embroidress. In addition Queen Elizabeth employed two hundred gentlemen, yeomen, officers and soldiers to guard her, the cost being approximately £50 a week, but was slow to reimburse the Earl. Mary was probably happiest at Chatsworth, which Lord Burghley referred to as 'a very neat house in good preservation.' From Chatsworth she was able

to visit Buxton where she took the waters and convalesced following an illness.

There were various attempts to free Mary, one of these involving Anthony Babington of Dethick, when she was imprisoned at Wing-field Manor in 1586. Because of the responsibility, the Earl was fully pre-occupied with Mary and this gave

The monument to Bess of Hardwick (1520-1608), designed by herself, which stands on the south wall of the Cavendish Chapel in Derby Cathedral.

Barlborough Hall, built in 1583/4, anticipates features incorporated in Wollaton Hall and Hardwick Hall. It was built by Robert Smythson for Francis Rodes, Justice of Common Pleas in the reign of Elizabeth, one of the judges at the trial of Mary, Queen of Scots.

Elizabethan period and has an important place in County history.

It was the sixth Earl of Shrewsbury who was responsible for the raid carried out in 1587 by Roger Columbell, the steward of Haddon Hall, with about twenty soldiers, on a mansion at Padley where John Fitzherbert was believed to be hiding two Roman Catholic priests. No trace of the priests could be found because the household had been warned by a relative, Robert Eyre. Unfortunately John Fitzherbert's third son, Thomas, informed the Earl of what was happening and a surprise raid on 12 June 1588 discovered the two priests, Nicholas Garlick and Robert Ludlam, hiding in a fire-place in Padley Chapel. The priests were tried at Derby and found guilty under the Act of 1584 and sentenced to be hanged, drawn and quartered and their bodies placed on poles at the approaches to St Mary's Bridge.

Three years before this the Grammar School at Ashbourne received its Charter with the first Head paid a salary of £20 a year plus a house and garden. He was able to supplement his income by taking in private boarders, but he had the strict instruction 'to avoid over-crowding with not more than two to a bed.' About this date, grammar schools were at Wirksworth in 1584, Dronfield in 1579, Staveley in 1586, and Risley in 1594. Earlier foundations were established at Tideswell in 1560, at Chesterfield by the gilds and charities in the fourteenth century, although the grammar school dates from 1598. Duffield in 1565, Repton under the will of Sir John Port in 1557, and Derby, where the school was refounded under the trusteeship of the bailiffs and burgesses of the town, in 1554.

A Derbyshire man to hold a high Office of State at this time was Sir John Coke who was the second son of Richard and Mary Coke of Trusley Manor. For twelve years he was a lecturer in Rhetoric at Trinity College, Cambridge, but in 1591, at the age of twenty-eight, he became liaison officer between Burleigh, the Lord Treasurer, and Greville who was Treasurer to the Admiralty. His brother wrote to him in 1601 from Trusley, 'I find now that you have

Bess an excuse to spread rumours at Court. As a result the Earl was relieved of his custodianship. Bess, however, had not endeared herself to the Queen by arranging the marriage of her youngest daughter, Elizabeth Cavendish, to Charles Stuart, Earl of Lennox, younger brother of Lord Darnley, who was Mary Queen of Scots' late husband. The Queen immediately ordered Bess to be sent to the Tower. Bess's husband, the Earl of Shrewsbury, nearly joined her but was able to persuade Elizabeth that he knew nothing of the affair.

Following her release from the Tower, a break with the Earl was inevitable and this led to a sordid squabble over the apportionment of the properties and goods, the squabble involving the tenants on the many estates. This undignified affair, which involved the Bishop of Lichfield and Coventry, was brought to an end by the Earl's death. At his

death it has been assessed that Bess had an income of £60,000 a year. In 1591, she travelled to London in a litter slung between four horses accompanied by several baggage wagons and forty-three attendants with church bells being rung in each village through which she passed. But her journeys to London were infrequent as she had so much to supervise at home.

The last eighteen years of her life were a great building period, during which she transformed most of her houses and built the second Hardwick Hall, the High Great Chamber of which Sacheverell Sitwell described as 'the most beautiful room, not only in England alone, but in the whole of Europe.' Bess, who Horace Walpole described as the 'Costly Countess', eventually succumbed on the 13 February 1608 at the age of eighty-seven. She epitomised the arrogant grandeur of the obtained that which you always courted, namely great and continuous business, and little leisure to attend to unnecessary matters . . .' In the previous three years he had been overseas, during which time the Navy had deteriorated as a result of graft, corruption and maladministration. Coke was appointed to hold an enquiry into the state of the Navy and his findings revealed 'no man is preferred for merit but for means only.'

Following a period in which he lived as a country gentleman in Hertfordshire, he was called upon to join another Commission set up in 1618, to inquire once again into the chaotic state of the Navy. The Commission found that ten ships of the fleet of thirty-three were 'wholly decayed and fit for firewood.' As a result of their findings, the members of the Commission, under John Coke, became a permanent Board, which in five years was able to have in service thirty-five ships with a further ten under construction. They also trimmed the cost of running the Navy from £53,000 a year to £35,000.

For his efforts Coke received a knighthood in 1624, a few months after the death of his first wife. He bought the Rectory at Melbourne in 1628 and proceeded to develop it as a comfortable country house for his newly-married son. Coke was a man of integrity with no political views 'except for a fixed dislike of anything that smacked of Papacy.' It was this Puritan streak which turned Queen Henriette Maria against him, and as a result Coke was dismissed from his office as principal Secretary of State to Charles I in 1640. Coke retired to Melbourne, only to be caught up in the Civil War, during which the Royalist soldiers gave him little peace. To escape their attention, he sought the security of his London home in January 1644, to die there that October.

Opposition to the oppressive taxation of Charles I is shown in the County's response to the Benevolence of 1626, when four of the Derbyshire Hundred Courts refused to pay anything to the Crown and only £20 4s (£20.20p) was raised in the whole County instead of the anticipated

The Pavilion designed by John Smythson for the Harpurs of Swarkestone Hall and built 1620/22.

several hundred pounds. In 1634, the King attempted to raise ship money from the inland counties, Derbyshire's share being assessed at £3,500 to provide for a ship of 350 tons with a complement of 140 men. Derby's share of the total was fixed at £120, until the new High Sheriff of the County, Sir John Gell of Hopton, informed the Secretary of State that the citizens were able to bear between £250 and £300. As a result, Derby's levy was raised to £175, but in fact the people of the town refused to pay anything. Chesterfield followed suit so that by 1637 Gell had with difficulty raised only £60 from the whole County. He had Sir John Stanhope of Elvaston arrested for failing to pay, distrained his goods, and had his

cattle impounded and allowed to starve, although by law it was forbidden to seize animals. This would appear to have been a personal grudge because Gell was less strict with other defaulters. In 1635, Charles visited Derby when he made the Town Council lend him £300, a loan which was never repaid.

The Civil War broke out on 22 August 1642 when Charles raised his standard at Nottingham Castle. The following day he set out with his troops for Shrewsbury, staying overnight in Derby where he slept in 'a great house in the Market Place'. Charles only managed to enlist twenty men in Derby, reflecting the lack of enthusiasm for the King's cause. The Royalist families who supported the King included Everys of Egginton, Fitzherberts of Tissington, Gilberts of Locko, the Hunlokes, Cokaynes, Harpurs, Vernons and the Cavendishes. The County was largely Royalist especially in the north and west and provided the King with eight regiments of horse, foot and dragoons. These did not cancel out the strong Roundhead position under the leadership of Sir John Gell of Hopton, who was supported by the Mundys of Markeaton, the Hortons of Catton, the Curzons of Kedleston, the Burdetts, the More-woods and the Wilmots.

The town of Derby was occupied by the Parliamentarians in January 1643, and remained so for the whole War. It is interesting that it was the same Sir John Gell of Hopton, who had raised his force largely at Chesterfield, and who was in command of the regiment which held Derby, who was the Sheriff responsible for attempting to raise ship money from the town on behalf of the King. In July 1643, Gell besieged and captured Wooton Lodge, which had been fortified by Sir Richard Fleetwood, and held by 'a company of obstinate Papists and resolute thieves, as the like were hardly to be found in the whole Kingdom.' Soon afterwards a 'battle' took place at Hartington in which the Royalists succeeded in taking three hundred Roundhead prisoners, but these were soon liberated in a counter-attack by Colonel Gell. His next foray was at Wirksworth in October where about three hundred of his men scattered the Royalist force. Early in December and in January 1644, he attacked Sir John Harpur's house at Swarkestone, and fought a fierce skirmish at the Bridge.

Until this time the Parliamentarians had been successful locally but then the Earl of Newcastle's Royalist forces entered the County and pillaged their way almost to the outskirts of Derby. However the Royalists under Colonel Dalby were besieged by Gell at Wingfield Manor for three days, when the garrison of Wingfield, as well as those at Bolsover and Chatsworth, were captured. Soon after this, Cromwell ordered the demolition of Wingfield Manor and Eastwood Hall.

In the same year a Royalist force

The porch of Chapel-en-le-Frith Church, built in 1733 by Platt of Rotherham. The first church was a chapel for the foresters of the Forest of the High Peak (1225).

was ambushed near Tissington, but reassembled at Burton upon Trent only to lose an entire detachment under Colonel Eyre in the church at Boylestone with Gell's men 'so taking men, armes, collours and all without loss of one man on either side.' But not all battles were bloodless. Colonel John Meynell, a Royalist, was killed at Burton Bridge.

Tutbury Castle was a Royalist garrison under General Hastings, and Charles visited it in August 1643 with the survivors of the Battle of Naseby. A few days later, the force marched to Ashbourne, beating off an attack by Colonel Gell's men at Sudbury. In Ashbourne Church Register it is recorded 'King Charles came to the church and many more and talked with Mr Peacock' who was the vicar. The King passed through the County again in August 1645, when he stayed at Chatsworth *en route* from Ludlow to Welbeck.

The year 1646 saw little organised fighting in the County, but the Parliamentary troops mutinied because they had not received regular pay, and plundered the countryside. It appears that bands of Royalists had been doing the same thing.

In 1643, Colonel Hastings, who was operating in Leicestershire, made a declaration forbidding looting by his troops and threatening death to anyone who took horses, money or goods to the value of two pence in Leicestershire or Derbyshire. He assured merchants that if they brought their goods to Leicester to sell, their horses would not be seized 'as was lately donne at Derby to the grosse prejudice and terror of his Majesties subjects.'

The Civil War resulted in the curtailment of trade at the Derby Horse Fair. In 1642, 290 horses had been sold; in 1643 only 36, in 1644 there were 43 sales but in 1646, 701 sales were recorded. Two years later, following the defeat of the Scottish army under the Duke of Hamilton at Preston, some 1,500 prisoners were brought south to Chapel-en-le-Frith. There they were kept in the small church for sixteen days, and as a result of the over-crowding forty died, with the remainder in a pitiful condition when they were released.

Two members of the Council which sentenced the King to death in 1649 were from Derbyshire families; Bagshawe, the President of the Council, and Ireton, who was Cromwell's son-in-law.

Thirty-nine years later another Derbyshire man was to have a hand in a change of monarch. By 1688, James II had antagonised many of his subjects. The suspicions that Charles II, who was a professed Protestant, had been taking secret communion with Rome, was also aimed at James II. In his three years as King, James completely sacrificed any hold he had on the country by his continued flouting of Parliament, by his intrigues with France, and by the horror of the 'Bloody Circuit' presided over, in his name, by the Judges Jeffreys and Kirke. The time was ripe for intrigue. One of the conspirators was the Earl of Devonshire who was a consistent opponent of both Charles II and James II. At the time in question, he was exiled from court as a result of a 'scene'. The Earl of Danby, Mr John D'Arcy and the Earl of Devonshire met at Whittington when, as the Earl of Danby wrote, 'we were partners in the secret trust about the Revolution.' Tradition has it that the three met during a hunt on Whittington Moor at the 'Cock and Pynot' which was an inn on the edge of the Moor.

As a result of the meeting a formal invitation from seven of the leading men in the Kingdom was sent on 30

Ashbourne Market Place showing horse sales in the early twentieth century.

June 1688 to William of Orange. In support of William, the Earl of Devonshire marched from Chatsworth to Derby with 500 men and invited all the chief townsmen to dinner, but he was coldly received, so much so that John Cheshire, the mayor, refused to billet the troops, and therefore the Earl went on to Nottingham where he was better received. As a result of the part he took in establishing William and Mary on the throne, the Earl of Devonshire received a Dukedom.

Perhaps the most dramatic event in Derbyshire's history occurred some fifty-seven years later, when Prince Charles Stuart, grandson of James II, marched south into England, having set up the Stuart standard at Glenfinnan on 17 August 1745. The 'Young Pretender' marched from Carlisle to Stockport and then headed for Derby through Macclesfield and Leek.

Tradition has it that the Prince stayed overnight on 3 December at Ashbourne Hall, the home of the Cokaynes, and the following day he lunched with German Pole at Radbourne Hall, having been proclaimed King at the Market Cross in Ashbourne. At this time the Duke of Devonshire was reviewing at Derby '660 men lately raised by subscription of the Gentlemen of this Town and County besides about 120 raised by His Grace and kept by his Grace at his own expense.' This body of armed men, along with Derby gentlemen and tradesmen, left the town before the vanguard of Bonnie Prince Charlie's army reached Derby at about eleven o'clock on the morning of 4 December. An eye-witness wrote: 'At the same time the bells were rung, and several bonfires made, to prevent any resentment from them that might ensue on our showing a dislike of their coming among us.' Two of the Prince's officers demanded 9,000 billets of the townsfolk. The main body of the army marched into the town in mid-afternoon 'in tolerable order, six or eight abreast, with about eight standards, most of them white flags with a red cross; their bag-pipers playing as they marched along.'

On their arrival, it was reported in the *Derby Mercury*, which missed one edition, that the troops were given bread, cheese, beer and ale. The Prince 'arrived in the dusk of the evening and he was billeted at Lord Exeter's residence.' The proclamation of the Prince was made in the Market Place by the Town Crier before he arrived, but it was reported that the Prince 'looks very much dejected . . .not a smile being seen in all his looks.' Such artillery as the rebel force had was assembled on Nun's Green, the commonland for the townsfolk.

The rebel troops seem to have behaved fairly well though there were the usual complaints about their drunkenness and petty thieving, particularly of footwear. There appears to have been little looting, but many horses were seized in the town and surrounding countryside. During the day an advance guard moved south to occupy Swarkestone Bridge, the only bridge crossing of the Trent between Burton and Nottingham, a government spy reporting that the force was between 400 and 500 strong; in fact it was between sixty and eighty.

On the morning of Thursday, 5 December, a Council of War was held at Exeter House, and it was at this gathering that the Young Pretender heard of the reluctance of his officers to move south into the lowlands of England, the doubt about French support, the disagreement between the Scots and the Irish, the lack of support from the Derbyshire families, the Harpurs, Burdetts, Poles and the Stanhopes, and the lack of fresh troops from Scotland. In all it was a gloomy picture which was sustained with false information from Hanoverian spies. According to Lord Elcho, the Prince was furious and 'fell into a passion and gave most of the Gentlemen that spoke very abusive Language, and said that they had a mind to betray him . . .'

At a second Council of War, he accepted that retreat was inevitable, saying, 'In future I shall summon no more Councils, since I am accountable to nobody for my actions, but to God and my Father, and therefore I shall no longer either ask or accept advice . . .' On the morning of 5 December, the Scots called for money from the citizens of Derby, including a half year's Land Tax and £100 from the Post Office. In the afternoon High Mass was said in All Saints Church. On Friday 6 December, 'at 9 o'clock, their Prince, being well-mounted, set out from my Lord Exeter's House, went over the Market Place, up the Rotten Row, and down the Sadler's Gate on the way to Ashbourne', with the Highlanders believing they were moving south.

The inhabitants of Melbourne in fact were prepared to receive the Pretender's army on the Friday night, *en route* to Leicester, at the time some of the retreating troops on the road to Ashbourne were making a well-behaved visit to Kedleston Hall, from where they took 'the two old brown mares, Miss Glanville, and out of the Coach House Stable, Old Bully . . .' The visit to Okeover Hall, where they ransacked the cellars and took horses, was less well-disciplined.

Only three Derby men had joined the Pretender's army — a blacksmith, a butcher, and a framework knitter — and they soon deserted.

Following the retreat, the life of the Town and the County settled down to normality once again with the return of the Smiths, Bakewells, Franceys and Gisbornes, along with the Mayor. This was to be the last major interference in the daily activities of the people of the County, but the divided loyalties of the Civil War were reflected in the division between those who adhered to the Church of England, and those who were Dissenters. Similarly, the arrival of Bonnie Prince Charlie relit the antagonisms against the Recusants who were persistently punished for their beliefs.

Parliamentary representation for the County after 1734 was dominated by the Cavendish family, who usually held one of the seats voted for by an electorate of about 3,000. The second County seat was held by one of the other gentry, usually a Curzon, but at times a Harpur or a Mundy would be elected. The Cavendishes stood as Whigs and the Curzons as Tories. The Borough of Derby, with an electorate of about 700 voters, returned a Cavendish and a Stanhope (the Earls of Chesterfield) between 1715 and 1748. Elections were open affairs, the votes being registered outside and recorded in the Poll

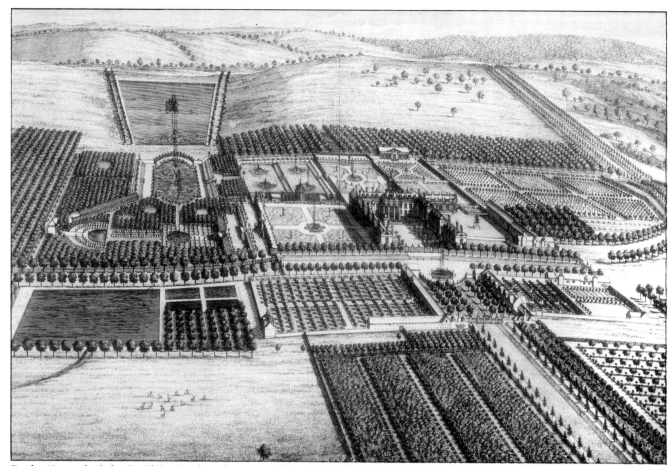

Bretby House, built by Sir Philip Stanhope between 1610 and 1616. Baron Stanhope of Shelford (Nottinghamshire) 1616, became the Earl of Chesterfield in 1628. Celia Fiennes visited the house in 1698 to see the gardens and waterworks laid out by the Frenchman, Grilly. Disliked by the fourth Earl, his cousin, the fifth Earl, had it demolished in 1780. The present house by Jeffrey Wyatville was started in 1813, being completed after some years.

Kedleston Hall designed by Mathew Brettingham c.1758 with centre portion re-designed by James Paine in 1761 who handed over to Robert Adam, for Sir Nathaniel Curzon, first Baron Searsdale, to replace Smith of Warwick's red brick building.

Books, and naturally voters were subject to bribery, drink flowing freely at election time.

Seventeenth-century Derbyshire was considered by Southerners as not pleasant to live in. Pepys recorded on 3 November 1662 that the Duke of York 'is smitten in love with my Lady Chesterfield' and so much that the Duchess of York 'hath complained to the King and her father about it'. On 19 November he wrote, 'Lord Chesterfield's going and taking his lady from Court,' . . .and . . .'did presently pack his lady into the country in Derbyshire, near the Peake; which is become a proverb in Court, to send a man's wife to the Peake when she vexes him.'

Hidden Treasures

THE eighteenth century saw a marked increase in the exploitation of Derbyshire minerals. Minerals have been worked since pre-Roman times, and include lead often in association with zinc and silver, iron, coal, limestone, gritstone, gypsum, clays, sands, gravels, fluorspar and barytes. The workings of these rocks and ores have scarred and continue to despoil the Derbyshire landscape whether in the vicinity of the Peak Park or in the southern lowlands.

Evidence that the Romans worked the lead deposits is to be found in the pigs of Derbyshire lead which have been discovered, but exactly where the lead was quarried or mined is not known. From the abbreviated inscriptions on the pigs of lead, the Roman mining centre, if there was such a place, was *Lutudarum*. There is no clear evidence that the Romano-British lead industry continued into Anglo-Saxon times, but it is presumed that lead was worked by the Saxons because in AD 714, mines at Wirksworth were in the possession of the Abbey of Repton. Lead to the value of three hundred shillings was sent to Christ's Church, Canterbury, from Wirksworth as a condition of tenure. The mineral rights ultimately passed to the Crown.

In the Domesday Survey, Derbyshire was the only County with a record of lead production, information being given for 1066 and 1086, suggesting a continuity from before the Conquest. The lead ore was obtained from shallow surface workings which followed the lines of the principal veins, or 'rakes', in the

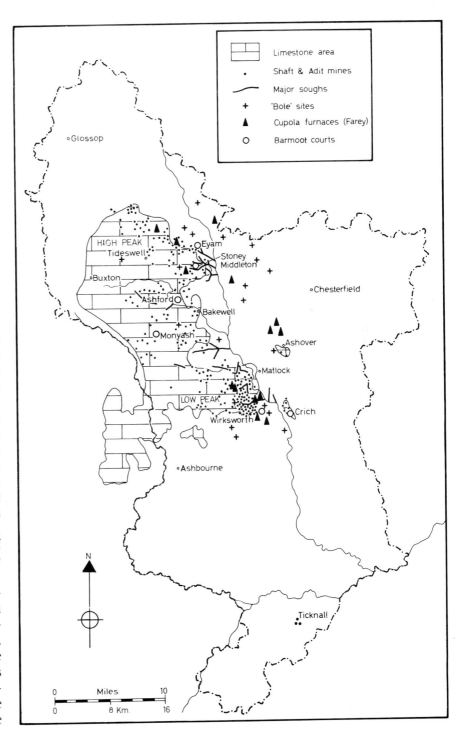

	Limestone area
.	Shaft & Adit mines
	Major soughs
+	'Bole' sites
▲	Cupola furnaces (Farey)
O	Barmoot courts

Glossop

HIGH PEAK
Tideswell
Eyam
Stoney Middleton
Buxton
Chesterfield
Ashford
Bakewell
Monyash
Ashover
Matlock
LOW PEAK
Crich
Wirksworth
Ashbourne

N

Ticknall

Miles
0   10
0   8 Km.   16

Lead workings along the White Rake near Wardlow.

The Magpie Mine near Sheldon which is drained by the Magpie Sough to the River Wye. Probably worked for over 300 years. In 1824 a Newcomen Atmospheric Engine was installed by Joseph, son of Francis Thompson. In 1833 there was trouble between Magpie and Maypitts and Red Soil miners. In 1872, Magpie was the third greatest lead producer after Millclose and the Bage Mines. In 1962 it became the Field Centre of the Peak District Mines Historical Society.

limestone upland manors including those of Wirksworth, Crich, Ashford, Bakewell, Matlock and Hope. It would appear that the lead ore was smelted in the manorial smelting hearths or boles, thus giving the Lord of the Manor a monopoly of the production of lead.

The Inquisition of Ashbourne, held in AD 1288 to determine the rights and customs of Derbyshire lead miners working on the Royal lands, known as the King's Field, established that mining customs had been handed down from 'time out of mind'. This customary right is reflected in the power of the Barmoot Court which oversaw and still oversees the lead-mining operations, even outside the Common Law as it affected the rights of the land-owner.

An official, with the title Barmaster, which may be of Saxon origin, was appointed for each lead-mining district by the owner of the lead-mines, to hear claims, settle disputes, transfer ownership and to measure the ore produced, in order to assess the 'lot and cope', which were taxes payable to the Crown and the landowner. John Wall and other miners in the High Peak challenged the King's right to certain dues on the ore they extracted in the 1760s. Barmoot Courts were held at the Moot Halls, the chief ones being at Wirksworth for the Low Peak which continues today, and Monyash for the High Peak. It is interesting to note that during the early years of the fourteenth century, Derbyshire miners were press-ganged for work in the stannaries of Cornwall — as many as one hundred and twenty in 1309 and one hundred in 1319. In 1282/ 3, sixty masons, carpenters and diggers had been conscripted from Derbyshire and Nottinghamshire and sent to Chester to assist in the construction of the North Wales castles. Labour was mobile as later in history.

Evidence of the more extensive workings of the eighteenth and nineteenth centuries is to be seen in the hummocky landscape and the small stone huts or 'coes' which are to be found around Wirksworth, Brassington, Carsington, Winster, Elton, Sheldon, Eyam and Castleton. 'All the county is scoop'd by lead mines, and their levells: betwixt Winster and Elton are the great lead mines of Port-Way', wrote the Hon John Byng in 1790.

However, the lead mine owners employed only a few men on a part-time basis and paid them seven pence for a nine hour day. 'The miners employ those hours which are not spent in subterraneous work, or necessary refreshment, . . .in clearing the ground for the ploughs . . .', wrote Bray in 1777. The miners were usually poor but the lead merchants, who controlled the movement of the

lead from the mines to the smelters, there being fifty of these in the seventeenth century, and then to the markets, were affluent. The lead was carried by lines of mules or ponies (the Galloways), under the control of 'jaggers', to the markets at Derby and Chesterfield, whence it was sent to Hull. Fortunes were made out of the lead industry by the Gells, the Babingtons, the Manners, the Devonshires, and by the Ferrers in the south of the County in the vicinity of Calke.

Mining was carried out on a larger scale in the late seventeenth and eighteenth centuries, the industry reaching its peak in about 1750 when about 4,000 individuals, men, women and children, were employed. The London Lead Company first turned its attention to Derbyshire in 1720/ 21 when it took up the leases of several mines in the parishes of Wensley and Winster, where contemporary houses reflect the prosperity of the industry.

At this time mines were working to a depth of about 180 feet (54.86 metres) but ground water pre-

vented workings at a great depth. The driving of soughs to drain the water required the input of capital by the larger companies. The two and a quarter mile Yatestoop sough was driven between 1742 and 1764, at a cost of £30,000, to drain the mines in the Winster area. The oldest recorded sough, the Longhead, was begun by Vermuyden, the Dutch water-engineer in 1629 to unwater the Dove Gang mines above Wirksworth, but because of the unwillingness of the miners to pay the Dutchman, he left the work to be finished seven years later by John Bartholomew.

In order to mine at even deeper levels, waterwheel-driven pumps were installed to drain the mines, as in the Lathkill Dale mines, while in the late eighteenth century, steam-engines were introduced. The Cornish-type steam engines were the most popular and several of these were installed by Francis Thompson, the Ashover engineer. Gregory Hillock mine at Ashover produced £140,000 'without any expence to the Proprietors'. (Hatchett, 1796). The capital outlay and coaling costs

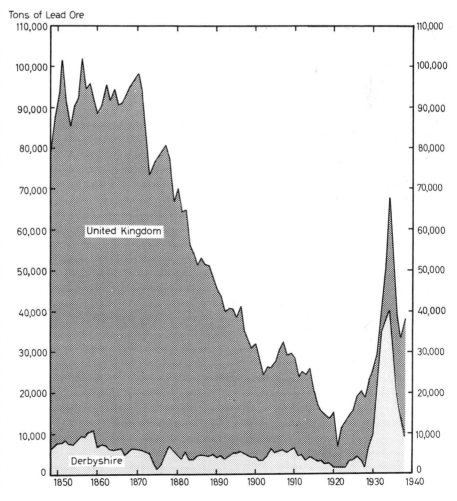

necessitated quick returns, and since the deeper ore levels tended to be of poor quality, companies soon found they were running at a loss. There was a bankruptcy sale of shares in 1811 which involved the lead-mines named Trafalgar, Gibralter, Perseverance, Ranter Tacker, Windmill, Quakers, Slack Rake, Hardnell and Bows Rake.

At the end of the eighteenth century production was between five and six thousand tons a year. The decline in ore production was reflected in the reduction in numbers employed in the lead industry, which by 1850 had fallen to about two thousand, and by 1900 fewer than two hundred were employed.

Mining methods showed few developments. As late as 1880 A.H.Stokes, the Inspector of Mines for the Midland District, stated that the methods used in the Peak showed little improvement on the 'old Saxon mode'. He knew of only two shafts where the miners' descent was mechanised; in the rest miners descended by ladders of even footholes and stemples, that is pieces of wood placed in the side of the shaft.

In the small mines most of the machinery was operated by horse or by manpower. The Mill Close mine at Darley Dale, which had been reopened in 1859 by E.M.Wass, was the only one to be worked on a large scale into the twentieth century. Following a period of decreasing production in the 1920s, a rich ore body was discovered and in the 1930s over 800 men were employed, but production at Mill Close ceased in February 1938 when water flooded the lower production levels, and although attempts were made to drain the workings, these failed and the machinery was sold in May 1945. Today the site is used for reclaiming the lead from vehicle batteries.

The smelting of lead in the early period was carried out in boles, that is hollows, sited on the south-west facing slopes and as Joshua Childrey wrote in the mid-seventeenth century 'they melt the lead upon the top of the hills that lye open to the West . . .' In the seventeenth century lead was smelted in furnaces with foot-operated bellows, these later being water-powered. It is possible that such smelting furnaces were introduced by German workmen because in 1692 a charter was granted to the London Lead Company which said ' . . .that they wish (to introduce) several furnaces, ways, engines, methods and means not hitherto found out or put in practice a very useful way of purifying and refining lead with pit coal and sea-coal.' The use of coke in the cuploa smelting process was recorded by John Martyn in 1729. White coal (dried chips of wood) was used in the eighteenth century in ore hearths with horizontal flues. In 1808 Derbyshire had about twenty lead smelt works mostly sited mid-way between the ore field and the coal-mines, but by 1870 there were only eight, these being of the open-hearth type. Smelt-works had to be sited with care as the fumes poisoned the land in their vicinity, resulting in animals suffering from the 'belland', that is lead poisoning. Industries associated with lead included red and white lead production, paint-works and lead-shot making. Today the lead mine spoil heaps and the old mines are being re-worked for the fluorspar and barytes which had been rejected as useless by the earlier miners.

There is plenty of evidence of the use of the varied rocks in the County in the numerous quarries. Landowners in the north and east of the County quarried gritstone, shales, limestone, coal measure sandstones and magnesian limestone in order to surround the fields laid out as a result of the enclosures of the late eighteenth and nineteenth centuries. Little is known of the builders of these walls but members of the Wagstaffe family built them in the Biggin-by-Hartington area in the 1800s.

The most important rock produced in Derbyshire today is limestone, the County accounting for about one-

Smelting House in Middleton Dale, from Chantrey's Peak Scenery.

The lead-mining village at Bonsall with its ancient cross in front of the King's Head (1677). Also, a framwork knitting centre, the houses had individual bridges to cross the stream that flowed through the village.

third of the total produced in the United Kingdom. It was first quarried in Roman times both as a building stone and for cement. The value of lime for improving the soil was appreciated by the end of the fifteenth century and at the end of the eighteenth century was in great demand. Farey, in 1809, mentions the eagerness with which limestone was sought for burning, and most farms had a small pudding kiln. Arthur Lowe, who produced the *Board of Agriculture Report on Nottinghamshire*, wrote on the uses of lime made by Coke of Pinxton. From 1793, Edward Banks & Co, under lease from the Butterley Company, carried limestone from the Hilts Quarry at Crich to wharves on the canals, where it was burnt in kilns for local consumption. The large lime kilns, which were built at Ambergate and Bugsworth alongside the canals, were connected with the respective quarries at Crich and Dove Holes by tramways. In 1808, from the tramway terminal at Bugsworth fifty per cent of the limestone was sent by canal to Bolton, Bury, Rochdale and Huddersfield for the textile and iron industries, thirty-seven per cent was

The Ashover Norman lead font, one of about thirty in the country and similar to the one at Doncaster.

distributed locally by cart and wagon, while the remainder was used for bleaching and cement making.

Samuel Oldnow erected lime kilns with a gothic façade at Marple Bridge alongside and below the Peak Forest Canal. One of the chief lime-burning centres was Stoney Middleton. Bray described the scene in 1777 as follows: '. . . over the town is seen the smoak of numerous kilns, used for burning the rocks into lime for manure

The reworking of fluorspar and barytes along the Deep and High Rake (1949). This has been reclaimed. Lead spoil is indicated by leadwort, alpine pennycress and moonwort fern.

The incline linking the Crich quarries with the Ambergate lime kilns, built by Stephenson in the 1840s.

The work force of Hilts Quarry, Crich, pictured in the early years of the twentieth century.

. . .These kilns . . .work only in the summer except one, which is constantly employed in burning lime for the smelting cupola (lead) here. It takes two days to burn a kiln; the lime is drawn out at Bottom and sold for two-pence a strike, or bushel. The men earn from eight to ten shillings a week. Small carts bring a load of slack from about Sheffield and Chesterfield and receive for it a load of lime.'

The numerous Ticknall lime kilns of Sir Harry and Sir George Crewe were equally important in the nineteenth century for the south of the County, being linked by a tramroad with the Ashby Canal (1802/03). Ninety-five per cent of this lime was used on the land.

In 1769 the proprietors of the Trent and Mersey Canal obtained the lease of a large tract of limestone at Caldon Low, and to obtain access to the quarry a canal was built in 1777 from Etruria Summit Lock to Froghall, where a plateway continued from Froghall Wharf to the Caldon Low quarry. The Cromford and High Peak Railway (1830), which was built to link the Cromford and Peak Forest Canals, gave an outlet for the limestone quarries in the Wirksworth area and at Grin and Harpurhill, near Buxton. Pilkington in *A View of the Present State of Derbyshire,* written in 1789, referred to people living in caves hollowed out of the huge spoil heaps of lime ash at Grin Low, and

Lime kilns in Middleton Dale (c.1815), from Chantrey's Peak Scenery.

Lime kilns in Great Rocks Dale, pictured in the 1960s. The houses were built by the Midland Railway. To the left was the Blackwell corn mill.

Aerial view of Middleton-by-Wirksworth in November 1957, showing the lead-mining hummocks. The field boundaries suggest enclosures of a small number of strips. The line on the left is the Cromford and High Peak Railway. In the centre is the limestone mine.

the successors of these 'troglodites' were recorded by Sant-Fond in his travels (1799), and were enumerated in the 1851 Census.

Sant-Fond described the habitations as having three or four rooms, 'almost all of a round form, for the purpose of solidarity . . .apertures are made by the door to admit a little light . . .but they are too poor to erect walls.'

The opening of the Midland Railway line between Rowsley and Buxton in 1863 gave faster, cheaper transport links for the quarries of Great Rocks Dale and Dove Holes as well as supplying the railways with ballast. Larger, more efficient kilns were built in the quarries alongside the railway lines. The branch line to Wirksworth gave access to the quarries in the area and to the unique limestone mine at Middleton-by-Wirksworth. The Wirksworth area along with the Caldon Low quarry producd 210,000 tons of limestone blocks for the construction of the deep water harbour at Port Talbot in 1967-8, and also for the Thames Tidal Barrage. Cement is produced at the works between Bradwell and Hope where both shaley-clays and limestone are worked in close proximity. The exploitation of the limestone has changed and is changing the topography of the County, although some of the earlier workings are being infilled.

Gritstone has been quarried for many centuries both as a building stone and for making grindstones. Like limestone, gritstone was used extensively for field boundaries and small quarries scar the fields of mid and north Derbyshire. Chatsworth House, the Crescent at Buxton designed by Carr of York in 1782, and numerous other houses, mill-buildings, farm buildings, stations, bridge abutments and viaducts are constructed of Derbyshire gritstone. The stone for Chatsworth as well as St George's Hall, Liverpool, was quarried at Sir Joseph Whitworth's Stancliffe quarry at Darley Dale. The quarries at Little Eaton and Cox-bench provided the stone for All Saints Church at Derby, Birmingham Town Hall, and Trent Bridge, Nottingham, as well as many of the stone-sleepers for the Butterley tram-

The Crescent and Stables, Buxton, pictured in 1910.

ways. The stone from Blue Mountain quarry, near Little Eaton, was used when the Peckwash Mill was rebuilt between 1810 and 1820. Huge gritstone blocks from the Derbyshire quarries provided the beds or foundations for the many steam engines erected in connection with the mining industry in the eighteenth and nineteenth centuries, and for the Howden and Derwent Dams.

As the name implies, the rock was an important grindstone whether for milling grain, pulping wood, crushing lead ore or sharpening edge tools and cutlery. 'Peak Stones' from Derbyshire, regarded as the best for flour-milling, were used in Thames-side mills in the fifteenth century, and relic quarries are to be seen on Stanage Edge, Stanton Moor, where a quarry produced millstones for the Far Eastern market into the 1960s, and Beeley Moor, which was famous for the fine-textured stones used in the needle-grinding industry, which was important at Hathersage (where there were thirteen millstone makers in 1590) in the eighteenth and nineteenth centuries.

Millstones were worked usually *in situ* by the stonemason and varied from 2 feet 3 inches (68.5 cms) in diameter by 8 inches (20.3 cms) thick

to 5 feet 7½ inches (171.45 cms), being priced from £8 to £20 per pair. An advertisement appeared in the *Yorkshire Herald* on 6 March 1790: 'J. & A. Lowe of Hathersage, Nr Dronfield, begs leave to inform their friends and the public that they make and sell all sorts of millstones from the same quarry that their late grandfather John Lowe of Calow had, which are equal, if not superior, to any millstones in England.' More recently, stone were cut using steam or diesel engines as the power source. Grindstones are produced at Birchover today and used by a file-making firm in Sheffield.

In the mid-eighteenth century cheaper, segmented millstones, made of a type of quartz, were introduced from the Continent, although known much earlier. These ground flour finer than the Derbyshire millstones. A side effect of the introduction of 'French' stones was that as a result of the poor harvests of 1755 and 1756, the price of flour rose above the pocket of the working man. By using the new stones, Mr Evans, a miller at Darley Abbey, openly boasted that £10 worth of corn could easily be ground into £20 worth of flour. The public, however, thought that this was achieved by grinding peas and

beans and even lime and plaster with the corn, all made possible by the newly-imported millstones! In September 1756, men of the Wirksworth area rioted and attacked several mills with the express purpose of destroying the 'obnoxious French millstones'. When the rioters marched on Derby, the militia was called out, and arrested six of them. However, the riots had little effect on the milling industry and gradually the French burr stones, imported at the rate of 27,000 per annum in the late eighteenth century, ousted the Derbyshire millstones, with the result that the local industry declined rapidly.

Other rocks mined or quarried in the County in the eighteenth and nineteenth centuries included 'black marble' from Ashford-in-the-Water, where Henry Watson worked the marble in his works alongside the River Wye in the second half of the eighteenth century at the site where Thornhill experimented with the water-turbine, and Blue John, from the mines in the vicinity of Castleton, the firm of Brown and Son originally of the Silk Mill and later of Bridge Gate, Derby, being a leading producer as was the Woodruff family of Buxton.

In 1784, it was observed that

Unfinished millstones on Millstone Edge, Hathersage.

Brown's retail shop was 'well-stocked with vases of every form and size as well as other works in fluorspar of different colours, but much better worked and of finer polish than those sold at Buxton and Castleton.' Grey 'marbles' were also produced from pockets of hard crinoidal limestone found at Sheldon, Monyash and Hopton and these are found in staircases and fireplace surrounds in houses throughout the County. Chert, mined at Ashford and Ashover, was used in the pottery industry.

In the south of the County, alab-aster has been worked from the gypsum pits at Chellaston and in the vicinity of Burton since the four-teenth century. The alabaster was used, in the main, for altar pieces and tombs. A feature of the work of the Chellaston 'kervers' like Pentrys and Sutton was the weeping or Lowick

An unfinished gritstone drinking trough on Hathersage Moor.

The alabaster tomb of Sir Ralph Fitzherbert (d.1483) and his wife in Norbury Church.

Sir Ralph's feet rest on a lion with the figure of a bedesman under his sole.

angels found on tomb chests. In 1408 a Royal passport was given, permitting an alabaster tomb to be exported to France to be placed over the grave of John, Duke of Brittany, at Nantes. Chellaston alabaster found its way into churches and cathedrals in France, Italy, Spain and Iceland, as well as locally, in the fourteenth and fifteenth centuries, when Burton upon Trent was a centre of the craft.

The decline in tomb-making following the Reformation resulted in the closure of the Chellaston quarries, although alabaster was transported by water to Wells on Sea for the interior of Holkham Hall and it is used locally in gardens as at Elvaston.

The industry enjoyed a brief revival when Sir Gilbert Scott used Chellaston alabaster for a reredos in Ely Cathedral and for the interiors of stately homes, but the quarries

Gravel working in the lower Derwent Valley, pictured in the 1970s.

Glass bottles were taxed until 1850, so making stonework bottles was popular. These were manufactured by Stirland and Company of Chesterfield and William Burton of Codnor Park. Burton was taken over by Joseph Bourne in 1833. The bottles are from the Roy Morgan Collection.

closed down prior to World War Two. Gypsum plaster was used in the pottery industry, and for flooring, and the white-washing of walls, but is not exploited in the County today.

Sands and gravels have been extracted over the last two centuries, particularly in the Trent and lower Derwent valleys, and today form the second most important extractive industry. One unusual industry was that of silica firebrick production at Friden, near Hartington, set up alongside the Cromford and High Peak Railway in 1892 and which exploited the sporadic pockets of glacially deposited silica sands in the area. Two kilns were erected alongside the railway line above Royston Grange.

Clay has been dug in the Brassington area in connection with the production of pottery and earthenware, and at one time (1775) was 'considered' by Wedgewood. Reference has been made to the manufacture of cooking-pots at Hazelwood, Holbrook and Derby during the Roman occupation. It is possible that tiles were manufactured in the Repton area in pre-Norman times, and there were mediaeval potteries at Burley Hill, Quarndon, at Dale, Melbourne and Ticknall. The works at Ticknall continued in operation

into the seventeenth century when Philip Kinder, writing in 1660, commented 'earthen vessels, pots and pancions are made at Tyknall and carried all East England through'.

Brownware, including bottles, was produced in several potteries in the Brampton area where there were at least seven in the nineteenth century. In the eighteenth century, earthenware was made at Crich, Wirksworth and West Hallam, where the earthenware pots for Strutt's fire-resistant mills were made, along with teapots and stoneware containers. Other potteries were set up at Belper by William Bourne and at Codnor Park by William Burton.

The purchase of the Denby clay workings was made by William Browne, who possibly had a pot-bank managed by a Mr Jaeger, but Joseph Bourne took over its operation in 1809. Soon after this date Shipley and Ilkeston potteries were established, as was the one at Langley Mill, about 1865, and the refractory and stone-ware producing works in the Swadlincote and Church Gresley area. In many of these areas bricks, terracotta, tiles and field drainpipes were produced. Tileyards were established at Staveley (1837), at Sutton-cum-Duckmanton (1826) and at Rowsley (1832). Woodville 'blues'

(tiles) were produced in the eighteenth and nineteenth centuries but eventually gave way to the cheaper slates brought into the area from North Wales.

One of Derbyshire's more important manufacturers is the Royal Crown Derby Porcelain Company which received the Royal Warrant in 1890. The early factory was located on Nottingham Road, Derby, in 1756, although creamware pots were manufactured on Cockpit Hill before this date and until John Heath's bankruptcy in 1780. The original Company declined and went out of formal existance in 1848, but a small number of employees moved into a house in King Street and continued as the Old Crown Derby China Factory. Thirty years later, the Crown Derby Porcelain Co Ltd was established and took over the old workhouse in Osmaston Road, where it is today. A china factory which was started at Pinxton by John Coke in 1795 and lasted twenty-three years, built up its reputation on the skill of the artist William Billingsley, who had previously been with the Derby Company.

The Growth of Industry

COAL occurs in three areas of the County: in the north-west on the slopes of Axe Edge, in the south around Swadlincote, and along the eastern half of the County from Unstone in the north to Stanton in the south-east. The earliest known reference to coal-mining in Derbyshire was in 1285, when an agreement was made whereby Hugh de Morley 'granted and confirmed to Simon, Abbot of Chester, free entrance and exit to his mines of sea cole wheresoever they may be found in his lands in Morley and Smalley (except through the long grass in the meadows, and the young corn) to all burgesses and sellers of coal.' This relates to Simon Field at Mapperley, near Ilkeston, which was worked until the early nineteenth century.

In the early fourteenth century, the canons of Beauchief Abbey were granted by Sir Thomas Caworth, 'license and full liberty of getting coals, drawing on them and carrying them away both for their own use and the use of their tenants . . .' At the same time there are records of coal being obtained at Swanwick, Morton, Wingerworth, Belper, Hulland Ward and Denby. Although most of the coal was obtained by opencast methods, some bell-pit working must have been used at Morley where in 1322 Emma Culhane was killed 'by the Damp while drawing water from a colepit.' Recent discoveries in the Coleorton area (then Derbyshire) show fifteenth-century long-wall working.

The problem of water flooding into the workings is highlighted in a reference to a pit in Morley Park in 1363 when a man was 'drowned for lack of a gutter', and accounts for the digging of drainage soughs. In the late fourteenth century, pits at West Hallam were leased by Ralph Cromwell and his son to a 'mining' consortium of men from Horsley, Horsley Woodhouse and Quarndon. The workforce was four pickmen and a waterpickman. The lease of 1398 permitted an extension of working into 'Symundfeld'.

During the Tudor period the requirements of the navy ship-builders for timber, and the growing demands of charcoal burners, as well as house building, resulted in a reduction of the acreage of home grown timber, and led to an increased demand for coal for home-heating as well as for various industrial purposes. When Sir Henry Sacheveral of Smalley stopped the transport of coal from Codnor through Kidsley Park in 1580; it was 'very hurtful to the inhabitants of Derby and places adjoining to have no passage for their coal and fuel', but it was the high cost of transport that prevented coal from the manor of Tibshelf in 1588 being sold in London in competition with sea-coal from the north-east of England, a problem which was to face Derbyshire coal producers until the mid-nineteenth century.

The sixteenth century saw the transference of the monastic coal-bearing lands of Darley, Dale and Beauchief Abbeys into other ownership but this did not stop exploitation continuing in a small way, as was the case in lead-mining. Coal-mining became more important in the County between 1550 and 1615, according to Professor Nef, in which period small collieries were started at Bolsover, Eckington, Wingerworth, Tibshelf, Totley, Chesterfield, Heanor, Langley, Stanley, Butterley, Swanwick, Duffield Chase, Belper, Denby, Shipley and Ripley and also in the south at Newhall, Swadlincote and in the vicinity of Staunton Harold and Coleorton.

The coal produced was used locally for malting, coal being exchanged for barley, which was in short supply in Derbyshire, from Leicestershire and Northamptonshire, for soap-boiling, Derby soap in the 1730s being considered as good as that of Bristol, and for lime-burning. It was suggested by Galloway in *Annals of Coalmining* (1898) that Derbyshire participated in the earliest attempts at smelting iron, using coal, but there is no evidence of this. However the exploitation of Derbyshire coal was restricted; as Kinder remarks in 1633, 'Here is no highwaies or post-waies . . .'

John Houghton described mining and drainage at Smalley about this time as follows: ' . . .my friend went down the pit twenty fathom, by ladders of twelve staves each, set across the pit one by another, when he was so deep he went underground (about half a mile) in a mine or vein which was about six foot, where were coals overhead and underground, the workmen knew not how thick: from this place he was led twenty yards through a narrow passage, upon hands and feet, till he came to a large space which was the head of a sough which laid all the pits dry that were on that land and presently he came to a pit twenty yards deeper than before, out of which they drew water brought from another pit twenty yards deeper with two vessels, which

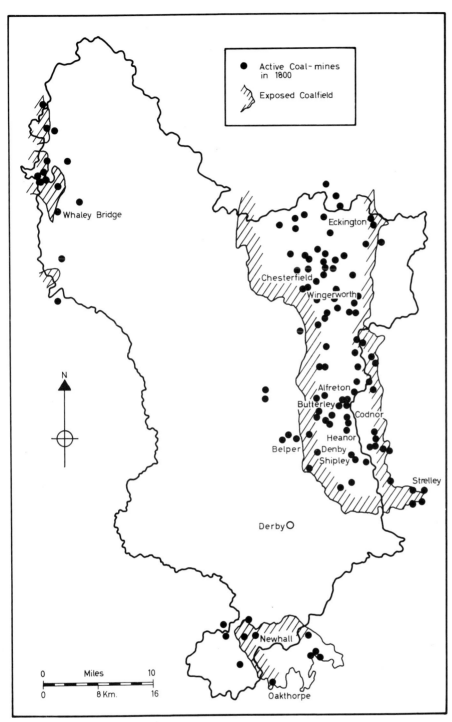

The coal mines c.1800 based on Nef and Farey.

would hold about sixty gallons each . . .'

During the eighteenth century the landowners of the County worked their minerals directly, or through salaried agents, or by letting part of them to entrepreneurs. The Devonshires had mines near Chatsworth and at Whittington, the Drury Lowes at Denby, the Mundys at Shipley, the Sitwells at Renishaw, the Cokes in the Pinxton area, while the Morewoods became involved in coal-mining in 1789 when George More-

wood, Lord of the Manor of Alfreton, acquired a Crown lease for 'the ancient mine at Swanwick' which had been in the hands of the Turner family since 1636.

In 1790 Benjamin Outram, in partnership with William Jessop, John Wright and Francis Beresford, established an ironworks and began to exploit the 'ancient coal' workings on the Butterley Hall estate. But some of the mineowners were humble yeomen and leasehold farmers like John Barnes of Barlow, who in 1763

obtained from the trustees of the Earl of Oxford the lease of a small colliery in the Parish of Staveley. From this small beginning evolved the Grassmoor Company.

Coke, which had been used since the early seventeenth century in drying malt in Derby, was used increasingly in the smelting of iron-ore in the latter half of the eighteenth century, and this expanding market for coal led to the development of the turnpike, canal and tramway networks. Farey wrote in the early 1800s: 'vast quantities of coals are annually sent out of the Counties of Derby and Nottingham southward by means of Cromford, Derby, Erewash, Grantham, Leicester, Melton Mowbray, Nottingham, Nutbrook, and Trent canals . . .' However, Derbyshire coal could not compete in London with sea-coal until the coming of the railways. At this time Derby, with a population of about 3,500, consumed about 5,000 tons of coal a year, costing 5s 10d (29p) a ton in the town compared with between 3s 2d (16p) and 3s 8d (18p) a ton at the pithead.

The increased depth of mining led to choke-damp and fire-damp becoming serious problems. The seventeenth century remedy for victims of the former was to 'dig a hole in the earth and lay them on their bellies with their mouths in it . . .If that fail they tun them full of good ale; but if that fail they conclude them desperate.' Explosions in mines were accepted as inevitable. Farey described how Joseph Butler of Killamarsh 'lays a slight tram-road along the bottom of the heading and keeps a pulley fixed in or near the forefield, over which a rope passes, so that when the accumulation of damp is suspected on the men's return to work, the tram can be drawn into the further end of the tunnel, carrying a lighted candle to light the gas . . .' Joseph Butler also placed a firebasket in the shaft in order to produce a flow of air round the workings. To cope with the problem of water, soughs were cut to supplement hand-pumps or horse-driven rag and chain pumps, but these were of limited value and by 1800 several of the larger collieries had a steam pumping engine, or fire engine, some of the engines having already worked at lead-mines. Farey also noticed over fifty winding engines, the first in Derbyshire being installed at Oakthorpe Colliery at Measham in 1790. Previously winding was done by horse gins.

At the end of the eighteenth century, a Derbyshire miner earned 2s 6d (12½p) a day, about four times the money an agricultural worker received. At Hasland Colliery the proprietor, John Brocksopp also owned a farm and he paid his colliers with farm produce, a version of the truck system of payment. Following the Napoleonic Wars, miners' wages rose to 3s 0d (15p) a day, but by this time the butty system was the pattern of working. The butty system was the outcome of groups of men contracting for a stint of work at a 'collective piece-wage' with the colliery manager. Inevitably this pattern of work led to the development of an 'underground hierarchy'. The Children's Employment Commission of 1842 reported that the coalmines in Derbyshire 'are wrought by butties who hire all the work people', and this system of coal-getting continued into the late 1930s. The same Commission established that more than sixteen per cent of underground workers in Derbyshire were boys under the age of thirteen. These boys worked a twelve hour day, five days a week, and from six in the morning to two o'clock in the afternoon on Saturdays, for a wage of between 8d (3½p) and 3s 0d (15p) a day depending on the job they did. The jobs varied from the opening of the ventilation doors to pulling corve-laden sledges, or leading the pit ponies.

Throughout the early nineteenth century the Derbyshire coal owners, such as Barber and Walker, Edward Miller Mundy, John Wright, Francis Wright, James Oakes, the Duke of Portland, Henry Case Morewood and D'Ewes Coke, sought to extend the market for the increased output which was being achieved by deeper mining techniques after *c.*1820. Although the Erewash Valley coal owners had attempted to get a railway built in the 1830s (the Midland Counties Railway), it was not until 1847 that the Erewash collieries obtained a rail outlet for their coals,

Clay Cross Company Ironworks, early 20th century.

Manner's Colliery (c.1907), Ilkeston. The Nottinghamshire and Derbyshire Electrical Power Company built a power station on this site to supply the town and the trams.

particularly to Leicester and Northampton.

George Stephenson, who had overseen the construction of the competing Swannington Railway by his son, constructed the North Midland Railway line which gave a southward outlet for north Derbyshire coal after 1840. During the construction of the Clay Cross tunnel on the North Midland line in 1837, Stephenson noted the rich coal seams and his exploitation of these gave rise to the Clay Cross Company. With the opening of the North Midland and Birmingham to Derby Railways it was possible to send coal to London by rail through Hampton-in-Arden,

although the first train loads had to be concealed.

In 1861 it was stated: 'The celebrated main coal of Clay Cross has attained such a decided position in the London market that the supply from the collieries is going to London, and until that market is satisfied no other can be supplied.' As a result of this exploitation of coal, Clay Cross, from being a small farming community in the 1830s, became a thriving iron-producing and coalmining community of over 6,000 in 1860, and by 1870 the collieries of the town were supplying one-tenth of all coal entering London by rail. From the mid-nineteenth century onwards

Coal measures landscape near Temple Normanton. Foreground shows typical rows of colliery houses. Middle right are brick and pipe-making kilns.

large numbers of deep collieries were opened particularly in the north-east, and the building of the Chesterfield-Sheffield line in 1870 led to an intensive exploitation of the coal in the Unstone and Dronfield districts.

The Midland and Great Northern Railway Companies competed to supply Derbyshire coal to the Metropolis, and this led to a price-cutting war which achieved almost economic suicide in 1871, after which date the companies agreed to charge an economic price for the carriage of coals. In 1872 nearly half of London's coal, which was carried by rail, came from Derbyshire. The GNR opened a line from Nottingham to Pinxton in 1874, and in 1878 from Derby to Nottingham, to capture the coal trade of the Ilkeston, Pinxton and Langley Mill pits, but Derbyshire mine-owners tended to remain faithful to the Midland Railway. Coal shortages and the price of coal at this time were usually blamed on the avarice of the mine-owners. The *Derbyshire Times* stated: 'So far as we know the coal and iron masters have taken very great care that for every extra sixpence they have paid their man, they have

charged the public an extra shilling ...', but the boom in coal prices ended in 1873 and prices were nearly halved by the end of the century. A general economic set-back in the last quarter of the nineteenth century resulted in collieries working three and four day weeks, and there were bankruptcies and pit closures. For example, J. and G.Wells closed two pits at Renishaw Park in May 1878, putting 600 men out of work.

Improved mining techniques were slow to reach Derbyshire. The first practical coal-cutting machine was used at Donisthorpe in 1861, while fan-ventilation was introduced by the Sheepbridge Company ten years later, although it had been used in South Yorkshire since 1852. John King of Pinxton patented a safety detaching hook for mine cages in 1867 and it was first tried out at Pinxton No 1 colliery in 1873.

The exploitation of the South Derbyshire coalfield took place much later than in the eastern area because of the lack of a nearby market and an adequate transport network, the absence of iron ore in the coal measures, and the non-coking properties of the coal.

The coal town of Swadlincote grew from a population of 216 in 1801, to 1,007 in 1851 and four times that in 1901. Such an increase was small when compared with that of Clay Cross or Ilkeston. Several of the large colliery companies built their own villages. The Butterley Company started to build housing at Greenwich (1804), Codnor Park (1810), Ironville (1811), Golden Valley (1813) and Hammersmith (1820); the Bolsover Company built Bolsover model village between 1891 and 1894, as well as Carr Vale and Creswell, while Hollingwood and Barrow Hill were built by the Staveley Company. In what was then South Derbyshire, at Moira, the Earl of Moira built Stone Rows (1811). In general the colliers' houses provided better living conditions than those experienced by other workers, particularly those in the textile industry.

Today the last three collieries — Markham, Bolsover and Shirebrook — operating within the County are threatened with closure. Derbyshire's hey-day for coal production was associated with the exploitation of the exposed coalfield, which is largely worked out and is now giving up its final offerings to open-cast activities. The spoil heaps of yesterday's mining are gradually being reclaimed and the ravaged landscape is being returned to farmland and leisure parks. The table shows the production of coal in Derbyshire:

Year	1808	1816	1841	1855	1906
Tonnage	269,456	942,218	1,500,000	2,256,000	16,567,209

The development of the iron industry in the County was closely associated with the exploitation of coal, the source of iron ore being in the coal measures black-band or from sandstone iron nodules, which averaged an iron content of about 30 per cent. Apart from the mention of a smith at Thulston and Elvaston in the Domesday Survey, there is no evidence of iron-working until the twelfth century when a charter of the Cistercian house of Louth Park in Lincolnshire refers to a gift by Robert de Abbetoft to the monks, of two hearths or forges at Barlow, near Chesterfield. There is also evidence that iron was worked on lands belonging to the Abbot of Burton;

in the thirteenth century it was being worked in the High Peak Forest, while in 1267 a forge was in operation in Horsley Wood, which was part of Duffield Frith. Ten years earlier the accounts for the Belper Ward of Duffield Frith show a return of £38 2s (£38.10p) from four forges, and there is visual evidence of the sites of early smelting-hearths on the west-facing slopes of the Ecclesbourne valley. There is also a reference to 6s 8d (33p) being paid for repairing the ways between Shottle Park and Postern Park for the carriage of charcoal to the lord's forge. In the north of the County, the monks of Beauchief Abbey were working iron and coal at Greenhill and Norton, and there were forges in the Scarsdale Hundred.

As was the case in the lead industry, work in the iron industry was on a seasonal basis, in addition to which the workers appear to have had frequent holidays. A return for two forges in Duffield Frith, for the thirty-four weeks from the Monday after Candlemas until Michaelmas in 1314, shows that there were fourteen days' holiday when no work was done. During the Middle Ages, Derby was the chief market in the County for the iron industry. Iron Gate was the street where small iron goods were manufactured and where one John, son of Peter le Parchemeyuer, held a messuage in 1348 'by the yearly rent of two pen-knives price one penny'. Ashbourne also appears to have had an iron industry, as an inventory of 1334 for the Tower of London itemises twenty small knives from the town.

The mediaeval industry was largely controlled by the larger land-owners. Lord de Grey, of Codnor Castle, had coal and iron mines in the area which passed by marriage in the early sixteenth century to the Zouch family, who in 1596 bought the Manor of Ripley from the Crown. John Zouch borrowed money at ten per cent from the Willoughby family of Wollaton who, when Zouch got into financial trouble, took a twenty-five year lease of 'the ironworks or anie of them, with the colepitts or myne of coles'. There are also references to the Zouch's operating forges at Makeney, Loscoe and Hartshay. In

The petroleum industry started in the UK in 1847/8, at New Deeps Mine, Alfreton, where James Young refined crude oil. This century, oil was pumped here at Hardstoft.

Robert Bakewell's (1682-1752) birdcage-shaped pergola in the gardens of Melbourne Hall. In 1708, Sir Thomas Coke's wife wrote: "Mr Bakewell has finished your work — and has had twelve pounds to pay for iron which must be stopped in your payment. He has got a workshop in Derby, but is so miserably poor that I believe he cannot remove till he has some money.'

the latter part of the seventeenth century, Sir Francis Willoughby of Wollaton had ironworks at Duffield where 105 tons of metal were cast in a period of eighteen weeks, and for which the founder received one pound a week, a high wage for the time, while the finer and hammer-man were paid 16s 0d (80p) for every ton of finished bar iron. At this time it is estimated that the Willoughbys' Codnor Works was producing two hundred tons of bar iron a year.

The Derbyshire iron industry developed rapidly in the seventeenth century, particularly in the north-east of the County. The Earl of Shrewsbury, in the late sixteenth century, had brought over Flemish refugees, and settled scythe makers at Norton and sicklemakers at Eckington. He built a furnace at Barlow, and to celebrate the event gave each of the workmen three pots of ale. In 1606, the iron mills on the Foljambes estates in the Dronfield area were assessed at 'better than £300 annually'. In the second half of the seventeenth century the Sitwell family came into prominence as iron-masters, having a number of forges and furnaces in the Renishaw area where saws, pots, pans, brewers' squares, nails, and sugar stoves and rollers for the West Indies were produced. In 1664 they supplied slit iron at £14 10s (£14.50p) a ton to John Finch of Dudley. The Sitwells also supplied the navy with £5,000 worth of iron bullets, which were delivered to Hull via Bawtry in October 1665. It was George Sitwell who complained about the demands made by the navy for the best timber, resulting in him having to search far and wide for wood for charcoal-making for smelting the ore. These forges and furnaces used water-power for driving the furnace bellows and the hammers which were sited alongside streams at Cuckney, Foxbrooke, North Wingfield and Pleasley.

The shortage of fuel and the inadequate transport network brought about a decline in the Derbyshire iron industry in the early eighteenth century, so that by 1750 there were only four forges working in the County, producing a mere 650 tons of bar iron annually out of a United Kingdom total of 17,350 tons.

It is not certain when coke was first used for iron-smelting in the County, but by 1788 there was only one charcoal furnace in use, which, with eight coke-fired furnaces, mostly in the Rother valley, produced 4,200 tons of iron annually. One of these, built by Francis Hurt of Alderwasley at Morley Park, where an iron-ore pit was sunk, in 1780, was possibly the first Derbyshire furnace to be blown by cylinder (steam) bellows. Farey wrote at the beginning of the nineteenth century: 'until about 40 years ago small furnaces and bloomeries heated by charcoal of wood, were alone used for the making of either cast or bar iron in these districts. At Wingerworth a charcoal furnace continued in use intermittently, blown by means of a water-wheel until the year 1784, when it was replaced by a coke furnace, this having been used more than 180 years. Farey lists twenty-three places where he had seen slag, indicating the locations of old bloomeries and charcoal furnaces.

Coke blast-furnaces were located at Wingerworth (1782), Staveley (1786),

Derbyshire Iron Producers

	1796 (a)			1806 (b)				1848 (b)			
Blast Furnaces	Furnaces Built	Pig Iron Produced (tons)	Operated By	Furnaces Built	In Blast	Pig Iron Produced (tons)	Operated By	Furnaces Built	In Blast	Pig Iron Produced (tons)	Operated By
Derbyshire Totals	12	9656		17	11	9074		30	20	95160	
United Kingdom Totals	131	125000		216	161	243851		623	433	1998568	
Alfreton (Chapel?)	1	1456	Saxleby & Co	1	1	1450	Saxleby, Edwards & Co	3	3	6240	Oakes & Co
Butterley	1	936	Outram & Co	2	2	1766	Butterley & Co	3	3	9880	Butterley Co
Chesterfield (Griffin?)	2	1560	Eb Smith & Co	3	2	1700	Eb Smith & Co				
Chesterfield (Stone Gravel)	1	940	Top & Co	2	1	700	Top & Co				
Clay Cross								2	(2)	8320	Stephenson & Co
Codnor Park								3	3	10920	Butterley Co
Dale Abbey	1	443	English & Co	2	0		A.Raby				
Duckmanton (Adelphi)				2	1	900	Eb Smith & Co	2	(2)	8320	Elsom & Co
Hasland (Park?)	1	853	?	1	1	723	John Brocksop				
Morley Park	1	728	Francis Hurt	1	1	420	Francis Hurt	2	2	4680	Mold & Co
Newbold								1	(1)	4160	Schofield & Co
Renishaw	2	705	Appleby & Co	2	1	975	Appleby & Co	2	1	4680	Appleby & Co
Stanton								3	3	10400	Smith & Co
Staveley	1	761	Ward & Lowe	1	1	596	Ward & Lowe	4	3	8840	Barrow
West Hallam								2	(2)	8320	Whitehouse
Wingerworth	1	1274	Jas Butler	2	1	819	Jas Butler	3	(2)	10400	Yates

() Temporarily out of blast.
Sources: (a) MacNab, vid, Nixon F.
(b) Reports from Commission on Mining Districts 1839-49.

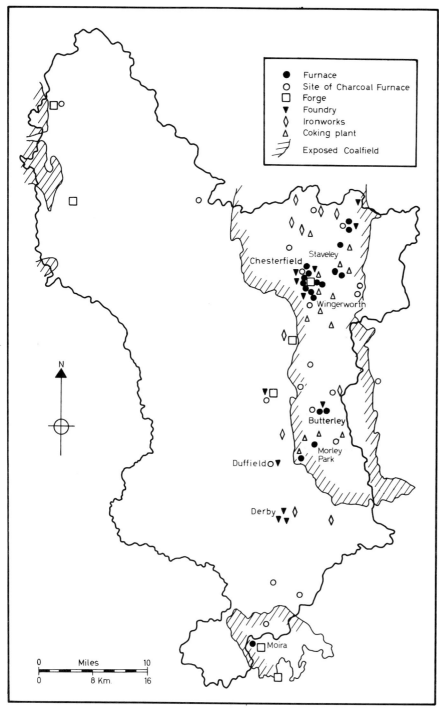

Iron-working activities in the early nineteenth century (based on Farey).

turn of the century, Derbyshire was the fourth largest producer of pig-iron in the country after Stafford-shire, Salop and Yorkshire, and of the County's total, the Butterley Company produced about a fifth.

During the eighteenth and nine-teenth centuries there was a wide variety of industries based on iron including nail-making at Belper, nail rod being delivered by Charles Hurt, Chesterfield, Derby, Eckington and Wirksworth; spurs at Bolsover, chains at Dronfield, Killamarsh, Openwood, Duffield, Measham and Unstone; needles at Hathersage, Ilkeston, Brampton and Derby; steam-engines at Derby, Butterley and Chesterfield; cutlery at New Brampton, Dronfield, Unstone and Derby; screws at Hartshorne; scythes at Norton, and sickles at Eckington and Barlow. The smaller articles were usually made by smiths working in small forges in out-buildings adja-cent to their homes, there being plenty of evidence of these in the hearth tax returns for the villages in the vicinity of Sheffield. Like the framework knitters, the smiths had a stint of work which they completed as and when they wished. Such a workforce was vulnerable to fluctua-tions in trade, this being the case with the Belper and Wirksworth nailers in the 1860s and 1870s following the introduction of the 'tommy hammers'.

Between 1830 and 1851, the iron industry expanded, largely as a result of the introduction of the hot-blast method of smelting, which lowered fuel consumption. By 1869 forty-three furnaces in Derbyshire were producing 188,000 tons of pig-iron, which was about ten times the 1830 output. Much of the pig-iron pro-duced was made into slit and bar iron and was finished elsewhere, partic-ularly in the Black Country, the canal network being important for its distribution. But Derbyshire pig-iron was not suitable for steel-making, and there was no large steel producer except Wilson Cammell at Dronfield (1873 to 1883), who made rails. Many Derbyshire firms like Weatherhead, Glover and Co, established in 1818, and taken over by Andrew Handyside in 1848, Derwent Foundry (1819), Eastwood and Swingler (merged

Dale (1788), Butterley (1791) and Riddings (1797). William Jessop of Newark wrote on 13 December 1788: 'I know of no better situation for establishing considerable ironworks . . .' with reference to Butterley. The Smiths at Chesterfield, who had the Calow iron works, the Griffin Foundry and the Adelphi Works at Duckmanton made ovens (1778) and cast cannons which were fired at the Battle of Ushant (1799), the iron columns for Strutt's West Mill at Belper, which was built in 1798, and

manufactured pumping engines to the design of Boulton and Watt, such as that installed in 1791 at Pentrich Colliery by Francis Thompson. In 1846, Benjamin Smith and his son Josiah were granted by the Earl of Stanhope a lease of ironstone, coal and fire clay in the parishes of Dale and Stanton-by-Dale, and so estab-lished the Stanton Iron Company. In 1877 this became the Stanton Iron-works Company, a firm which was operated from 1861 by Crompton and Company, the Derby bankers. At the

HANDYSIDE PILLAR BOX DESIGNS
after J. Farrugia

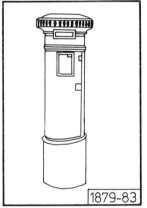
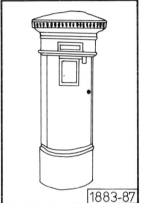

1864), Leys (1874), Butterley, Staveley, Stanton and James Oakes at Riddings concentrated on cast and wrought iron products including bridges, post boxes, lamp standards, fountains, stoves, mile-posts, rails and pipes, and latterly castings for the vehicle industry. Cast iron pipes were first manufactured in Derbyshire at Clay Cross in 1864, although they had been made at Coalbrookdale in the early eighteenth century.

The expanding industry resulted in the growth of built-up areas on the coalfield. For example, Whittington Moor, which had been a waste area, grew from a population of 870 in the 1850s to 5,578 in 1871, while between 1871 and 1881, Dronfield grew from 3,253 to 5,169, largely due to the expansion of the iron-producing companies.

During the 1870s local iron ore was unable to supply the demands of the industry and was supplemented by the Jurassic ores from Leicestershire and Northamptonshire, made accessible by the building of the Midland Railway line. From supplying forty-

The Butterley-built bridge for the Midland Counties Railway from Long Eaton to Loughborough, erected in 1839. The canal boats are crossing the River Trent from the Erewash Canal to the Soar Navigation.

Gallows Inn Ironworks, Ilkeston c.1905.

The Great Northern Railway and the Nutbrook Canal carried raw material to Stanton ironworks (1910).

two per cent of the County's iron ore requirements in 1872, local ore declined to two per cent in 1884. During this period, new blast furnaces were built near the railway at Denby (1860), Ilkeston (1863), and Awsworth (about 1880), but in general the Derbyshire iron works, which produced low quality pig-iron, did not keep abreast of techno-logical advances and this resulted in the closure of many of the smaller, inefficient units which were frequently out of production, by the end of the 1920s. Rationalisation took place in the industry, particularly in the period following the Second World War. Stanton took over Oakes' Riddings works in 1920, closing it in the late 1960s, while the works at Staveley were closed down in 1930, followed by those at Sheepbridge in 1970. In 1926 the Butterley Company abandoned its blast-furnace plant, and more recently the Clay Cross Company blew out its blast furnaces in 1958, followed by Stanton on 29 March 1974. The increasing cost of transporting the iron ore, and later the coking-coal, meant that the

Stanton Ironworks in the 1930s.

Derbyshire iron-industry was no longer competitive, and the various companies therefore diversified into pipe production and various forms of engineering, particularly after the coming of the railways.

One of the basic products of mediaeval Derbyshire was wool, and in 1809 John Farey referred to eighty farmers having white-faced wood-land flocks in the north-west of the County, the wool from which being for 'the hatter's use', by such as the Jenkinson's of Dronfield, and at Chesterfield in Beaver-Place, and for carpet-making. Chapel-en-le-Frith was important to the farmers of the Peak for its wool fair, and during the eighteenth century the weaving of wool was a household occupation in the Glossop area, where weavers' windows can still be seen at Hayfield, but weaving was generally important throughout the County. In the eighteenth century, Huguenot refugees brought their spinning and weaving skills to the area, and evidence of this activity can be seen on tombs in Darley Dale churchyard, and in inventories. The 1620 inventory of

Robert Mower, a yeoman of Milne-thorpe in the Parish of Dronfield, itemises six spinning wheels and a quantity of wool, but no loom.

During the eighteenth century most villages in the east and south of the County had some framework-knitting machines, their initial presence being largely the result of knitters leaving the London area to escape Guild restrictions. These machines which were built by local framesmiths, were based on the stocking-frame invented by William Lee of Calverton, Nottinghamshire, in 1589. This frame was improved in 1758 by Jedediah Strutt of South Normanton which enabled ribbing, 'the Derby rib', and therefore better-fitting stockings, to be made. In his appearance before a Committee of the House of Commons on 8 June 1779, Anthony Ryley of Alfreton reported that: 'A new Coarse Frame is worth 13 guineas — a new fine one is worth 15 guineas. A new Coarse Frame will go 10 or 12 years without a Recruit . . .I can undertake to keep those frames in repair for 8s a year . . .' Framework-knitting was a home-based industry and therefore did not suffer from the constraints of factory discipline, but during the eighteenth century the knitters came increas-ingly under the control of master hosiers who owned the frames which they rented to the out-workers. Such a man was William Muggleston whom Ryley reported as having served his apprenticeship in the trade and who owned about fifty frames. Thomas Kirk, who sold his fourteen worsted stocking frames in 1786, had frames at Derby, Ireton Wood, Chad-desden, Hill turnpike near Chester-field and at Horsley.

The frame-owners, and the bag-men who operated from a warehouse and who delivered the yarn and collected the finished product, levied a high fee for their services. Ryley continues: 'It must be a very good Hand to earn 8s a week. The Deduc-tions are rather better than Two Shillings which come out of that Eight . . .' The machines were either placed in attic rooms with long windows as at Ashford and Crich, or in ground floor rooms as at Hol-brook. As the industry evolved the machines were transferred from the

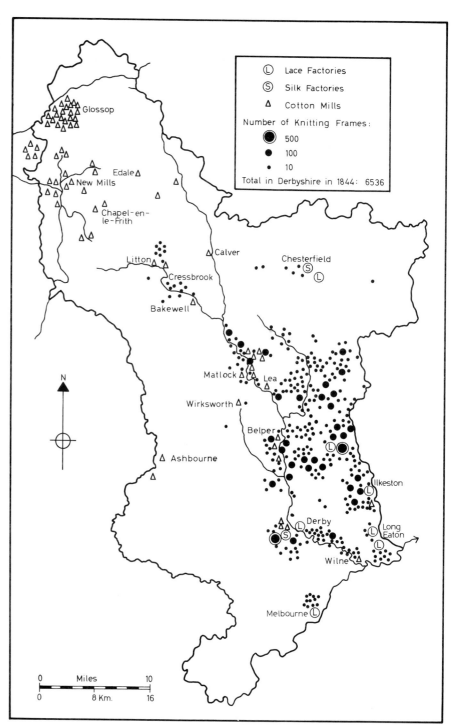

Textile activities in the eighteenth and nineteenth centuries.

houses into outbuildings added to the house, or placed in the gardens. In 1794 stocking makers at Ilkeston 'each had a garden, a barrel of home-brewed ale, a workaday suit and one for Sundays and plenty of leisure, seldom working more than three days a week'. These were the days of affluence for the framework-knitters, but it was not always so.

The master hosiers gave rise to the establishment of hosiery firms, like Brettles of Belper. Ward, Brettle and Ward was established in 1803 as a

London firm with a Belper ware-house whence yarn was distributed by bagmen to the framework-knitters in their homes, living within a radius of about twenty miles. By 1824, Ward, Brettle and Ward owned 269 stocking frames in the Belper area and had assets of £176,000. William Ward's death in 1833 resulted in the disso-lution of the partnership and George Brettle established the hosiery fac-tory, built originally as a warehouse. One employee was James Smith of Milford, who was recruited by the

Framework knitters' Apprenticeship Indenture for Joseph Shardlow — 30 November 1753 — for seven years.

firm along with his frame in June 1828. His son, Edward worked for Brettle's for eighty-eight years, starting at the age of ten. When he was ninety-six he was offered a generous pension but refused it, replying that if they could not find him work, he would get another job! Many hosiery firms were established in the early nineteenth century, including Longdon's in Derby, where a quarter of the machines 'were working with silk', and I. and R. Morley in Heanor, Thomas Haimes in Melbourne, who was an agent for Strutt's cotton thread, Beardsley's at Ilkeston and Smedley's at Lea. During the later part of the century, improvements to knitting machines resulted in the industry becoming factory-based, although outworkers still produced cotton, woollen and silk stockings

and gloves, and were involved in finishing processes such as seaming and chevening, the latter being the embroidering of a pattern along the dart of the stocking.

Like every other industry, the hosiery trade had its unrest. In 1911 there was unrest over the wages being paid at Lea Mills, a situation largely instigated by the Heanor and Ilkeston Workers' Union. At the time the employees at Lea Mills worked a forty-nine and a half hour week, which compared favourably with fifty-four and a half hours in most other factories. Ninety-five years before this there was one particular event which did involve the discontented framework-knitters. Changes in fashion at the beginning of the nineteenth century had resulted in a

reduction of demand for the Derby rib, and this and the general lack of work, together with the economic problems of the period following the Napoleonic Wars, led to sporadic outbreaks of machine-breaking among framework-knitters — the so-called Luddite Riots. In fact the Derbyshire framework-knitters were fairly peaceful compared with those of Nottinghamshire.

The year 1816 was cold and wet, with snow as late as June in Derbyshire, no growth of grass until the end of June and in the higher parts of the County, oats were not cut until October. Sir Henry Fitzherbert wrote: 'In consequence of all this a third of the working population were thrown out of employment and became paupers' and therefore were a severe drain on the resources of the parishes.

Lombe's silk mill alongside Cotchett's.

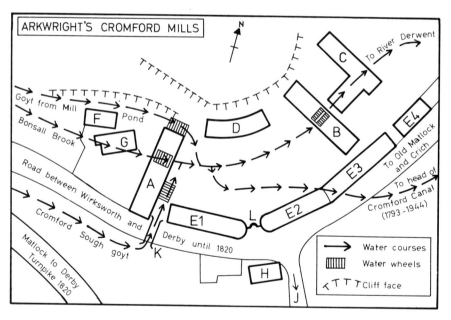

Arkwright's textile complex at Cromford.

A — 1771 mill with extension
B — 1777 mill
C — 1790 paper-making mill.
D — semi-circular building — offices?
E1-4 — Warehouses 1785-1795.
F — Offices

G — Counting house
H — Manager's house
J — Access to White House, the Arkwright residence
K — Aqueduct
L — Entrance to the mill complex behind which was
    a small check-in building.

Out of work hosiers would walk from Sawley to Heanor to get work. Fitzherbert went on to comment that crime had increased fourfold with the result that the prisons were over-crowded and, not unnaturally, various political societies were formed although most of their actions had been made illegal by the Government. One of those who spoke out against 'the Establishment' at this time was the Derbyshire Member of Parliament, Sir Francis Burdett of Foremark Hall. Because of the state of lawlessness, Habeas Corpus was suspended in March 1816. In an attempt to put their case to the Government of the day, the unemployed in Lancashire held meetings, as a result of which, a march on London was planned in order to petititon the Prince Regent. The peaceful March of the Blanketeers was halted by troops, and the last remnants of the marchers were eventually turned back at Ashbourne.

In the Alfreton and Ripley area there was similar discontent led by a local reformer, Bacon, a non-militant who became involved with militant reformers in Nottingham. As a result, it was arranged that the more militant Jeremiah Brandreth, who was a framework-knitter, was to return with Bacon and meet a group of men at The White Horse in Pentrich. At this gathering Brandreth, known as the Nottingham Captain, revealed a plan for a rising against the Government. The Government already knew of this

The Cromford Mill (1771) wheel-powered by sough water carried by the aqueduct.

plan through an informer, and as a result, local troops and the magistrates were prepared for the rising, which included a plan to take the Butterley Foundry. In the event this was thwarted by the manager and a few of the workforce. The undisciplined rebels marched toward Nottingham by way of Ripley, Codnor and Langley Mill, several of them defecting *en route*. News that Nottingham had been taken encouraged the rebels to press on, but at Eastwood, learning that troops were moving against them, the group threw down their arms and scattered. They were chased and some of the rebels were arrested, including Brandreth and his lieutenants Turner, Ludlam and Weightman. Following their trial in Derby, Weightman was transported and the other three were hanged and beheaded. The part taken by the Government in causing these men to be exposed was never made

clear but its authority was strengthened as a result of the incident. What is clear is that the men of Pentrich and the surrounding area were as reluctant in their support for Brandreth, as they had been reluctant to join the Pentrich and Ripley Volunteers, when they were formed in 1803-04 to defend the County against the possibility of a Napoleonic invasion.

The hosiery industry required large quantities of wool, silk and cotton thread. To meet some of these requirements Thomas Cotchett, in 1702 set up Dutch silk-throwing machinery in a three-storey mill on the River Derwent at Derby, with machinery driven by a thirteen and a half feet waterwheel, built by the eminent water-engineer George Sorocold. The works were expanded between 1717 and 1720 by a five-storey mill, which housed machinery manufactured to the pattern of

Italian machines, under the oversight of John Lombe, the son of Sir Thomas Lombe, a Norwich silk merchant. The Derby silk mill, which in 1732 employed three to four hundred workers, established the pattern of factory work, which was described vividly by Hutton in his *Autobiography*, for the next two centuries. The silk mill was the focus of interest for visitors to the town, but not always with enthusiasm. Viscount Torrington (Byng) writing of his visit to the mill on 19 June 1790, said 'The Silk Mills quite bewildered me; such rattlings and twistings! Such heat and stinks that I was glad to get out . . .', but he was an exception. A request by Lombe to renew his patent in 1732 was turned down, and a cash award of £14,000 was made to him. Following this there was a rapid expansion of the silk industry. In 1789 the town had twelve silk mills which employed

North Street, Cromford.

one thousand two hundred workers, but by then Derby and Chesterfield had been replaced as the main silk-producing centre by the towns of Macclesfield and Congleton. The silk industry nonetheless continued to prosper in Derby, until it was over-shadowed by artificial silk shortly after the end of World War One.

Derbyshire's connection with the production of cotton thread dates from 1770, when Jedediah Strutt, who it is reputed invented the 'Derby Rib', and who had already built a silk mill in Derby, joined Richard Arkwright to exploit the 'water frame' roller spinning machine which had been patented in 1769. At the time Arkwright was operating a horse-driven cotton mill in Nottingham, but the power source was inadequate, and with Strutt and Samuel Need he built the water-powered cotton-spinning mill at Cromford in 1771. Why the site at Cromford was chosen is not clear but the availability of a water-power source originally used by a corn mill and a lead-smelt mill would have

been important when sites with expansion potential were at a premium. Six years later a second mill was built. An unknown visitor in 1800 commented: 'The introduction of the cotton manufactory here was a most fortunate circumstance for the poor inhabitants who through failure of the (lead) mines must without it or some other resource have either migrated or perished'.

A succession of mills was built along the River Derwent and its tributaries by Arkwright and Strutt, at Bakewell (1777), Belper (1778), Cressbrook (1779) and Milford (1780), and also at Ashbourne (1781). In 1781, the death of one of their sponsors, Samuel Need, brought about the dissolution of the partnership, each man going his own way. Both men continued to build mills, Arkwright with a variety of partners, such as Dale of New Lanark, became involved in expensive litigation in unsuccessfully attempting to protect his patent. He and his son greatly expanded the communities of Cromford and Scarthin with industrial

housing such as that in North Street (1777), built the Greyhound Inn (1779), the church (1797) and a corn mill and a bobbin mill along the Via Gellia, and they also established a market in the village after 1790, encouraging stallholders to attend, by offering rewards to the most regular attenders during the year. This was necessary because of the nearby competing markets.

Arkwright was concerned to a certain degree with the welfare of his workforce, but he was more anxious to enhance his own social position. He was made High Sheriff of Derbyshire in 1786, during which year he was deputed to give the address from the Wapentake of Wirksworth to George III, on the escape of the sovereign from an assassination attempt. Shortly afterwards the King knighted Richard Arkwright for his services to the community. The building of Willersley Castle was part of the image-making, but because of a fire which delayed the work, he died in 1791 before his new residence was completed. The character of the man

A	Original Weir 1775-6	I	Junction Mill 1808
B	First Mill 1776 rebuilt as South Mill 1812	J	Round Mill 1811
C	North Mill 1786 rebuilt 1804	K	School 1818
D	Long Row 1794-7	L	Christ Church 1849
E	West Mill 1795-6	M	Chimney 1854
F	Road Gangway 1795	N	East Mill 1912
G	Horseshoe Weir 1797	O	Warehouse & Shops
H	Reeling Mill 1808	P	Workers Houses

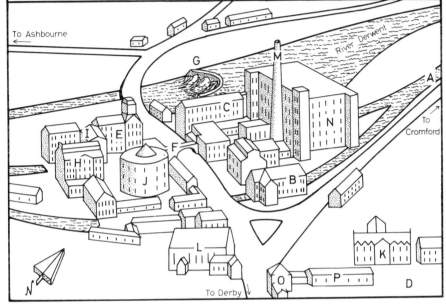

The Belper Mill complex.

The Belper Mill Complex (1992) and the Strutt housing.

is summed up in a letter written in 1786 by Mathew Boulton to James Watt: ' . . .If he had been a more civilised being and had understood mankind better he would now have enjoyed his patent. Let us learn wisdom by other men's ills'.

Jedediah Strutt's activities were concentrated at Belper and Milford, where extensive mill complexes were built by the Strutts between 1778 and 1827, and at Derby where his son William built his first fire-resistant building in 1793 based on an iron-framed construction. Of more advanced fire-resistant design was the Belper North Mill, built in 1803-04 to replace the original mill erected in 1786 and destroyed by fire. The Strutts had their own foundry at Belper, described by Elizabeth Grant in *Memoirs of a Highland Lady*: 'In this Cyclops den huge hammers were always descending on great bars of red hot iron, and the heat and the din, and the wretched looking smiths at work there made a disagreeable impression'. The many cast iron windows, to be seen in the houses built by the Strutts for their workers, were made at this foundry. Loudon cites such a house window costing 12s 4½d (62p) in the Appendix to his *Encyclopaedia*, and attributes their invention to Anthony Strutt. At the Milford Mills, William Strutt, who was an innovator, built a gasworks and also devised a system of ducted-air central heating throughout the mill. This system was later to be used in the Derby Infirmary (1810). He also provided a chapel, a reading room and a prison, and formed the 'Milford Militia' to protect the Strutt property against lawless marauding gangs of Irish labourers. Although the Strutts were fundamentally concerned with the welfare of their workers, their spartan Presbyterian upbringing made them hard task-masters. In the Belper area they established model farms, the produce being sold to the workforce in the mills and, like the Arkwrights, the Strutts became involved in both the political and social life of the County, particularly in the County town where they had a town house, now St Helen's House.

Many other cotton mills were built in the County. The mill at Calver was erected in 1776 by John Gardom

Strutt workers' housing, Long Row, Belper (1792-95).

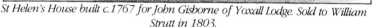

St Helen's House built c.1767 for John Gisborne of Yoxall Lodge. Sold to William Strutt in 1803.

Borrowash cotton mill. In 1789 there were five wheels used for corn-milling, slitting and tinplate. Cotton spinning from about 1800.

of Bubnell and his partner John Pares of Leicester and, like many other cotton mills, it was burnt down in 1802, later to be rebuilt. More recently, metal articles, including stainless steel hardware, were made at the mill by W. & G.Sissons Ltd of Sheffield. The Evans family, (the father was a partner in the Derby bank of Crompton Evans), encouraged by Arkwright, also a banker, built the cotton spinning mill in 1783 at Darley Abbey which became noted for its Boars Head sewing cotton. The family was also involved in corn-milling, iron and copper rolling and slitting mills, and in paper-making in Derby and at Darley Abbey where, like the Arkwrights and Strutts, the Evans family created a village community, taking good care to maintain their patronage and social superiority until the early twentieth century. While the Arkwrights and Strutts were early tycoons, the Evans were gentlemen factory owners. At Darley Abbey attention was paid, not only

Litton Mill. Built by Ellis Needham in 1782. Later under William Newton it employed 400 workers. In the 1870s fire destroyed most of the buildings.

to the material benefits, but also to the moral and spiritual welfare of the workpeople. A system of fines was instituted to discourage absence, swearing, and non-attendance at day or Sunday School, but for regular attendance throughout the year at Sunday School between 1890 and 1900, a person received 2s 6d (12½p) and four yards of calico. The fines were also used to help the sick and needy, who were visited by one of the ladies of the household.

Cotton-spinning mills, many built under licence from Arkwright, were also erected at Tansley, in Lumsdale, at Litton, Bamford, Darley Dale, New Brampton, Edale, Eyam, Little Longstone, Measham, Mayfield, Borrowash, Wilne and Lea, all between 1780 and 1820. In the north-east of the County, William Hollins established a cotton mill on the site of Pleasley Forge on the River Meden in 1784, although the present mill

buildings date from the 1840s. Hollins, in partnership with Charles Hill of Cromford in 1890, took over a garnetting mill in the Via Gellia whence the trade name Viyella was adapted in 1894. In the north-west of Derbyshire in 1790/91, Samuel Oldnow built a mill at Mellor (1790), at that time in the County area. The Arkwrights, who had given financial assistance to Oldnow, took over the mill on his death and ran it from 1828 until 1892 when it was burnt down. More than fifty cotton-mills were built during the years of the cotton boom, at Hayfield, Glossop and New Mills, and calico mills were established at Dinting in 1825, and along the valley of the Sett. Many of these were converted to printing and dyeing in the 1820s and 1830s.

Although the mills were originally sited on rivers and streams for their power-source, this usually proved to be inadequate and it was soon found

necessary to install steam engines, either to pump water for the water-wheel, or to provide the main power. The later canal-side locations were important for the supply of coal, and for a source of water, the local authorities at the time being unable to meet the water demands of industry.

The labour-force for the mills usually came from the locality, although Scotsmen were recruited at Cromford (1785), but mills in the more isolated places such as Litton and Mellor employed pauper apprentice labour. A prejudiced view of the conditions is illustrated by the story of Robert Blincoe, who was placed in the St Pancras Workhouse in 1796 at the age of four and later spent time in various cotton mills including Litton Mill. In spite of his disadvantaged origin he became a manufacturer in 1833. In the 1842 survey, the number of parish apprent-

The apprentice house at Cressbrook. William Newton built the original mill in 1783, but it was destroyed by fire in 1785. The Factory Inspector's report of 1811 said the apprentices 'looked well and appeared perfectly satisfied with their situation'.

ices claimed by cotton manufacturers in Derbyshire was as follows: Darley Abbey — 3 Edale — 31; Glossop (Mellor — 27; Worley Bridge — 2; Brokfield — 1; Wrens Nest — 1); Cressbrook — 66, but one can assume that these figures are on the low side.

Messrs Connel and Kennedy of Manchester purchased Cressbrook (c.1835) to supply the Nottingham lace market with cotton thread. It was at Cressbrook that the migration agent to the Poor Law Commission offered twenty young persons from the Kent Union of Milton, but when the time came 'all had found other means of support through family or otherwise.' The agent felt he had let down the mill manager (1836).

An apprentice who made good was Samuel Slater, who was born at Blackbrook in 1768. He was apprenticed to Strutt at the age of fourteen for a period of six years, during which time he promised to serve his master faithfully, to keep his secrets, to avoid fornication, matrimony, cards, dice tables and other unlawful games, taverns and play-houses. In return he was to be taught cotton-spinning and to be found meat, drink, washing and lodging. Having completed his apprenticeship, he left Belper for the United States of America where he managed the business of Almy and Brown at Providence. He found the machinery inadequate and set to work to build new machinery based on that he had worked at Belper. So was established Slatersville, a mill with a village similar to those at Cromford, and Milford (which was originally called New Mills), and Darley Abbey.

Hand-made lace was a product of the region in the eighteenth century, particularly of the Nottingham area, and a logical development of knitting hosiery by machine was to make lace-net on a machine. In 1808 John Heathcoat, son of a Duffield farmer, patented the bobbin-net machine, but his enterprise at Loughborough suffered from the attention of the Luddites. Because of this, Heathcoat moved to Tiverton but his partner, John Boden along with William Morley, set up a lace-factory in Derby in 1825. Other lace-factories using John Leavers' improvement to Heathcoat's machine, were built at Ilkeston (W.Ball and Son — 1825), Heanor (Fletcher — about 1845), Melbourne (Parker — 1860), Long Eaton (Bush and Austin — about 1840) and Chesterfield. There were c.300 bobbin-net frames at work in the County in 1836. Problems with labour in the Nottingham area in the 1860s resulted in some lace-manufacturers moving to Sandiacre, Long Eaton and Draycott, often renting standings in the large tenement factories which had been built by speculators such as Terah Hooley of Risley. Towards the end of the nineteenth century an observer wrote 'If those persons . . .think that by removing their machines to Long Eaton they will escape fierce competition, they are very much mistaken. Having recently paid a visit to that district I find that trade, generally is much worse than in Nottingham . . .'

Changes in fashion and the restriction placed on exports as a result of World War One, saw a rapid decline in the lace industry, with the result that many of the large tenement buildings were used by a variety of industries, making among other things, electrical parts, furniture and pianos. While lace tended to be concentrated in the south-east of the County, the Derby area specialised in the weaving of tapes and smallwares. This was introduced at the beginning of the nineteenth century and extended as far as Ashbourne and Wirksworth. James Smith & Co, which began a tailoring business in Derby in 1840, was noted for the making of uniforms.

Although the textile industry is no longer as important today as it was in the nineteenth century, small pockets of the lace-making, knitwear, hosiery and smallware industries continue today along with artificial fibre products, which have become increasingly important. The British Celanese works at Spondon, important for its Tricel fibres, was established in 1916 by the Swiss chemist, Dreyfus, to produce aeroplane dope, today is part of the Courtauld group. This was the year in which artificial silk was first spun at Dould's Spa Lane Mills in Derby, and a claim is made that Castle Mills at Melbourne was the first place in England to spin nylon thread. With the decline of coal-mining, the reclaimed colliery sites have provided locations for an increasingly important knitwear industry in the post-war period.

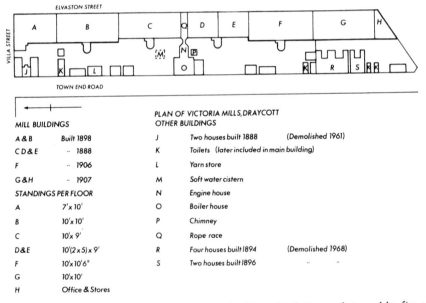

MILL BUILDINGS		PLAN OF VICTORIA MILLS, DRAYCOTT OTHER BUILDINGS		
A & B	Built 1898	J	Two houses built 1888	(Demolished 1961)
C D & E	" 1888	K	Toilets (later included in main building)	
F	" 1906	L	Yarn store	
G & H	" 1907	M	Soft water cistern	
STANDINGS PER FLOOR		N	Engine house	
A	7'x 10'	O	Boiler house	
B	10'x 10'	P	Chimney	
C	10'x 9'	Q	Rope race	
D & E	10'(2x5)x 9'	R	Four houses built 1894	(Demolished 1968)
F	10'x 10'6"	S	Two houses built 1896	" "
G	10'x 10'			
H	Office & Stores			

Victoria Mills, Draycott. A typical tenement lace building. Block E was destroyed by fire on 17 January 1902. Some fifty lace machines were destroyed.

Movement

THE inland position of Derbyshire made communications difficult and inhibited movement of the County's products far afield. The Romans were aware of the necessity for an efficient road network, both to dominate the countryside, and to exploit its resources. In order to develop minerals, eighteenth century industralists supported and often initiated travel improvements. Lord Macaulay wrote in the reign of James II: 'On the roads of Derbyshire travellers were in constant fear for their necks, and were frequently compelled to alight and lead their horses'. Other travellers such as Celia Fiennes and Edward Browne made similar comments. John Houghton stated that the cost of land carriage from Derby to the Trent at Wilden Ferry was the same as the water carriage from Wilden Ferry to Hull, ten times the distance.

The routeways that criss-crossed the County either followed the ancient ridgeways, sections of the neglected Roman roads, or the pack-horse tracks, which in places, as between Cossall and Ilkeston, and at Ashover, were paved with stone slabs, or followed holloways as between Morley and Stanley. The key to the routeway system was the point where the track crossed a river or stream in which the water level changed rapidly. The Prior of Repton was appointed surveyor of the bridge at Swarkestone in 1327, the bridge and causeway having been built between 1190 and 1204, when it was referred to as 'ponte de Cordy', while the

Packhorse track, near Barber Booth.

The 'new' St Mary's Bridge, Derby, with the Bridge Chapel of the fourteenth century bridge alongside. In the foreground is the Derby Canal link with the Derwent.

Abbot of Burton was responsible for the building of Monk's Bridge near Burton in the thirteenth century. The granting of pontage enabled those responsible for the bridges to collect tolls for their upkeep. This resulted in the erection of chapels on early bridges as at Cromford, Swarkestone and Derby. Responsibility for bridges passed in the sixteenth century to the Justices of the Peace through the Quarter Sessions.

Although responsibility for road maintenance had been placed in the hands of landholders by the Statute of Winchester of 1285, (in 1314 the good men of Ilkeston were granted pavage by Edward II) little was done to keep them in good repair. Therefore in 1555 the repair of the highways was made the responsibility of each parish and was supervised by an unpaid, elected Surveyor of the Highways, who was accountable to the Justices of the Peace at the Quarter Sessions, with each parishioner performing four days' labour on the roads per year, his statute duty. This was later increased to six days with the option of commuting to a cash payment, but this method of highway maintenance was not always effective. Eight parishes were brought before the County magistrates at the Easter Quarter Sessions of 1696 because, 'The King's Highway leading from Swarkestone to Derby is much out of repair so that His Majesty's subjects may not safely pass

on, by and over the same. Draynes and water courses are grown up with sludge and mire so that the water up on said (Sinfin) Moor could not have its free current and passage by reason where off.' The eight parishes had to pay 30s (£1.50p) each to Richard Sayle and Richard Sheppard 'who had to see to the draynes . . .' In 1665 the inhabitants of Markeaton were 'presented' for not repairing the road between Quarndon and Derby and the 'occupiers of Durleigh (Darley) for not repairing Frihers Lane'.

The Sheriff in 1664 — a Mr Ashton of Stoney Middleton — had no coach and when asked by the Judge why he did not bring one, replied that there was no such thing as having a coach where he lived 'for ye town stood on one end'.

In the early eighteenth century Revd James Clegg, a Nonconformist minister of Chapel-en-le-Frith, returning home from Buxton late one night, wrote in his diary ' . . .my mare boggled and started aside near Martinside, and ran headlong with me through deep ruts and stone pits a considerable way before I could stop him . . .' Leonard Wheatcroft, a parish clerk at Ashover, had experienced a similar incident in 1692, and was only saved from losing his way by following piles of stones erected by himself previously, Guide stoops at cross-ways were to be erected under an authorisation of Parliament in 1697 to indicate the nearest market

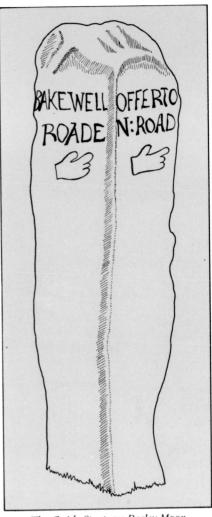

The Guide Stoop on Beeley Moor (Offerton = Alfreton).

town, but this was not acted upon by the Derbyshire JPs until 1709. An Act of 1835 instructed Overseers to the Poor to erect sign-posts at crossroads by 1 January 1836.

Glover in 1829 wrote 'In the Peak and Scarsdale districts, pack horses were anciently used for the conveyance of produce, ore etc, across the moors and dales', and some of the routes can be identified by the packhorse bridges, the holloways, the guide stoops, and by the Saltways. The importance of the Galloway breed of pony (under fourteen hands) as a packhorse animal which carried two to three hundredweight is reflected in the special races included for them in the race-meetings at Derby, Bakewell, Tideswell and at Winster in the eighteenth century. They were supplemented by cumbersome wagons, restricted to thirty hundredweight in 1662 (six tons in 1765) in the flatter south, some pulled by oxen, and to a lesser degree by carts

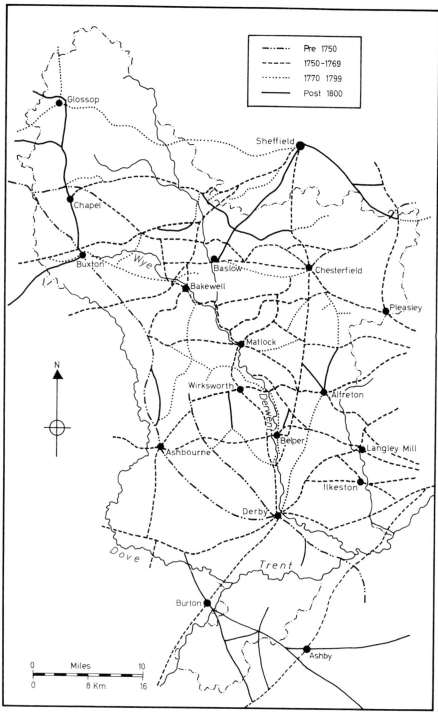

Turnpike Roads.

A comparison of the mileages turnpiked in Derbyshire, Nottinghamshire and Leicestershire. By 1750 only 13 miles of the 177 miles of the London-Derby-Manchester route was not turnpiked.

Mileages Turnpiked

	Up to 1720	1721-30	1731-40	1741-50	1751-60	1761-70
Derbyshire	—	10	65	15	242	120
Nottinghamshire	—	18	13	—	79	114
Leicestershire	—	27	12	—	196	74

by wagons to Southampton for export as early as the sixteenth century. More certain is the fact that imported goods were transported from Southampton to Leicester at this time, and to Derby.

In 1706/7 the first turnpike trusts were authorised, thereby removing the responsibility for certain stretches of road from the local justices, although statute labour was still used. The trusts were made up of interested parties, and those who wished to loan money on the basis of an annuity, usually five per cent. The earliest Derbyshire road to be turnpiked (1725) was the route along which Revd James Clegg had perilously travelled. This was followed in 1738 by the turnpiking of the road from Wilden Ferry (which was operated by an over-chain ferry) to Derby, where it divided, one route, the King's Highway mentioned in 1663, following the original highway to West Chester, through the parishes of Markeaton, Quarndon, Kedleston, Weston Underwood, Mugginton, Turnditch, Hulland, Hognaston to Brassington, from which point the road found its way over the limestone upland, the route being changed over the years and eventually falling out of use in places.

The other route went through Brailsford to Ashbourne, and on to Hurdlow House, a carrier's inn since the 1730s, near Buxton, by way of Mapleton, Thorpe, Tissington, Alsop-en-le-Dale and Hartington. This was amended in the 1760s by the route through Sandybrook and Red House, and in 1777 when the road was re-routed through Fenny Bentley. A new bridge over Shirley Brook was built in 1790/91 of two-carriage width. The improvement of the Loughborough-Derby road (1738) was probably in response to comments made to Parliamentary Commissioners by such as James Waddall of Nottingham, Ralph Skampton and Thomas Litchfield, who were carriers between Derby and London: 'They knew them to be very deep and dangerous...and with great difficulty escaped being hurt.'

Also in 1738, a short section of the road from Bakewell to Worksop, through Chesterfield, was turnpiked. This was important for the lead-

or sledges, which were used in the hillier northern parts. In the High Peak, a strong drag-chain was fastened at the top of the cart back to arrest their downhill progress.

The *Carriers' Cosmographie*

(1637) reported that 'the carriers of Derby, and other parts of Derbyshire, do lodge at the Axe, in St Mary Axe, near Aldermanbury, (London) they are to be heard of there on Fridaies'. It is possible that lead was carried

New Inns Tollhouse at the junction of Gag Lane and A515 — now demolished.

Coldwall Bridge over the Dove between Thorpe and Blore. On the Blythe Marsh to Thorpe Turnpike — 1762.

'very ruinous' and the trust was heavily in debt. Another turnpike to cross the County was that from Nottingham, through Alfreton, to Newhaven, was enacted in 1758. After this date, turnpike acts followed in quick succession. In 1791, Hutton listed eight turnpiked roads leading into Derby. It is important to remember that present-day roads do not always follow the line of the turnpikes, for some of them are today only tracks, as is the stretch of the original Ashbourne-Cheadle road between Thorpe village and Blore, over Coldwall Bridge.

Toll charges varied from one trust to another, and as they came up for renewal after twenty-one years, tolls were usually increased, being based on the number of animals needed to pull a vehicle or on the width of the fellies. On certain roads there were special rates for items like millstones, as in the case of the Nottingham, Ilkeston and Smalley Cross Roads turnpike. Trustees were invariably local landowners and prosperous merchants who had a vested interest in the road, and in certain instances the landowners owned the inns along the turnpike. Rarely, however, were they profitable enterprises, because of the need for annual payments, and the maintenance expenses. Toll-houses mark the sites of toll bars, but sometimes chains were placed across side roads, particularly where traffic avoided the toll-bars, this frequently being the case on the developing coalfield in the east of the County, where side roads crossed the turnpike.

As a result of these road improvements, traffic increased in speed and frequency. In January 1734, George Paschall, a Derby carrier describing himself as the 'old Derby carrier', advertised a wagon to leave Derby every Monday to arrive in London every Saturday and to return the following week. Another wagon commenced in May. Thirty years later, William Bass, who was to found a brewing enterprise, advertised that he carried goods between Manchester and London by way of Derby, but in a shorter time.

The Derby-London post service, at a cost of three pence (1½p), was established in 1635 by Thomas Withering, being confirmed by Acts

smelting house near Chesterfield as well as for the cross-country route to Manchester. In the *Journal of the House of Commons* for 1758 it was recorded that Joseph Burks, miller for twenty-five years at Tideswell, sent twenty horse-loads of meal and wheat flour each week to Manchester and had been doing so for twenty-four years. John Grundy of Baslow, Adam Barton of Padley and Isaac Metcalf of Over Water Mill near Chesterfield each sent fifteen loads a week. The same year, the surveyor for this road reported that six miles of it were in 'tolerably good repair' and the rest

Tollhouse on the Loughborough to Derby turnpike at the Aston-on-Trent junction.

Tollhouse at Stoney Middleton, built 1840/41 at a cost of £114 14s 0d.

of Parliament of 1657/60. The first identifiable postmistress at Derby was Mrs E.Reynolds in 1693. The Post Office was housed in a building attached to the George Inn, Sadler Gate, an important coaching house. Until 1784/5 all mail was carried on horse back by post boys (usually men), but in that year 'post coaches' were introduced.

The journey from Derby to London by coach took three days in 1757, reduced to one day in 1764 by the 'flying machine' so that by 1777 there was a daily service which cost £1 8s (£1.40p) for inside passengers, but was cheaper in summer than in winter and competition between coach proprietors became intense in the early nineteenth century. Coaches required frequent changes of horses at inns. The isolated Newhaven Inn was built in 1795 by the Duke of Devonshire because the Ashbourne to Buxton road was one of the most taxing for horses. Other inns on this road were the Dean of Harrington's Arms and the Bull i' th' Thorn, originally Hurdlow House. The better Derby-Leek-Manchester route was turnpiked in 1762 with many variations of route. The Peacock at Oakerthorpe, which was the post office for the Alfreton and Matlock area, was another coaching inn with extensive stabling.

More wheeled traffic meant the widening of packhorse bridges; accordingly, in 1777 the Quarter Sessions authorised the sum of £50 for the widening of the Cromford Bridge. Bridge trusts were set up to build bridges where ferries, which

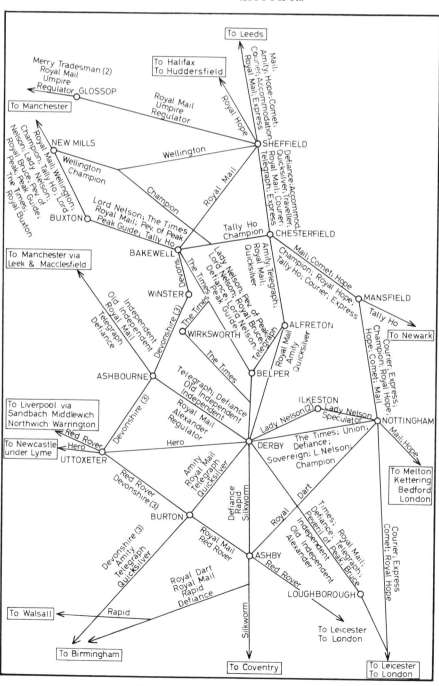

Stage coach routes in the 1830s.

Stage Coach Timetables for the London, Derby, Manchester Route

	1788 Bull and Mouth	1836 Swan with Two Necks
London	5.00am	7.30pm
London General Post Office		8.00pm
Islington (the Peacock)	5.51am	
St Albans	7.09am	
Redb(o)urn	7.31am	10.44am
Dunstable		11.32am
Hookcliffe	8.41am	
Woburn		12.27am
Northampton	Breakfast (20 min)	2.45am
Market Harborough	1.31pm	4.37am
Leicester	Business? (5 mins)	6.03am
Loughborough	4.03pm	7.30am
Derby	Dinner (20 mins)	9.07am
Ashbourne	7.11pm	10.25am
Waterhouses	7.45pm	
Macclesfield		1.13pm
Bullock Smithy (Hazel Grove)	10.40pm	2.03pm
Manchester	11.30pm	3.00pm
Total Time	18½ hours	19½ hours
Speed	10mph	9+mph

Stage coach timetables for 1788 and 1836.

Outside the Green Man, the coaching inn at Ashbourne. Robert Wallis was the landlord in the 1850s.

The Newhaven Inn (1795) replaced 'a mean public house nearly opposite the nine-mile stone' on the Ashbourne-Buxton Turnpike. Originally the Devonshire Arms, the name was changed when the Duke of Rutland acquired the estate on which it stands.

created bottle-necks, had previously operated. As a result Cavendish, Sawley and later Willington bridges were built in the latter half of the eighteenth century to replace ferries. The new St Mary's Bridge at Derby was built in response to the large increase in vehicular traffic. In a census taken on the old bridge for the year 1787, there were over 1,500 vehicular and 36,000 horse movements. However, the turnpikes were not a popular innovation. A toll gate at Far Laund, Belper, was pulled down and burned in 1797, perhaps a local example of the later Rebecca Riots.

Travel was far from comfortable. Jedediah Strutt's wife wrote in the 1760s 'At Glyn, six miles from Leicester I was so sick. I was not able to travel further, but staid behind the wagon more than an hour and then walked five miles before I came up with it'. A traveller in 1792 going from Duffield Bridge to Chesterfield by way of Higham wrote that the road was ' . . .so steep and difficult to ascent, that it is impossible for horses to drag their loaded coaches which pass that way; it is therefore common for the driver to request the passengers to alight; and I think it must be considerably above a mile that we walked before it became sufficiently level to take the coach again . . .'

As today, hostelries were good and bad. Celia Fiennes at Buxton in 1697 found 'the lodging so bad, two beds in a room, some three beds, and some four in one room . . .and sometimes they are so crowded that three must lie in a bed . . .' Viscount Torrington fared little better in 1789 when he stayed at the White Hart at Buxton, ' . . .neither I nor the beasts could eat the provender' but he found the Bell at Derby 'as good an inn as can be found amongst the bad ones in this town'. His opinion of the Rose and Crown at Shardlow was that it was 'just placed to my wishes, exactly different from The George at Derby; though the hostler being drunk and the women of the house sulky . . .'

Highwaymen made journeys hazardous. One highwayman operating in Derbyshire was Pierce Cook, who led a ruthless gang in the Derby area in the reign of George IV. One of his exploits was to set an ambush

The ferry at Twyford in the 1930s.

Clifton (Ashbourne) Tollgate.

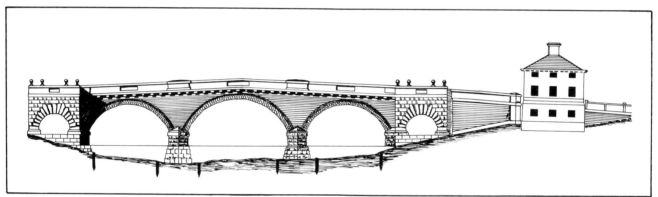

Cavendish Bridge, built 1758/9 by James Paine at a cost of £3,333 to replace the Wilden Ferry.

Willington Bridge and toll-gate built in 1839 by James Trubshaw to replace the ferry downstream.

on Cherry Tree Hill, Chaddesden, for R.S.Cox of Spondon Hall, who had been detailed to round up the gang with a detachment of the Derbyshire Yeomanry Cavalry. Cox managed to avoid the ambush, and Pierce Cook made his escape to London, where he was followed by Derby's solitary constable, who found him, arrested him and brought him back to Derby's town gaol in Friar Gate. One of the more successful hold-ups was in 1781 when two highwaymen took £1,000 from the Derby-Manchester mail coach. It was the railways more than the law that finished the highwaymen. The last Derby to Manchester coach set off from the Bell on 3 November 1855, although a coach continued to operate between Bakewell and Manchester by way of Buxton until 1858. Roads, however, were not an efficient means of transporting heavy goods. A table of alabaster taken from Nottingham to Windsor to be used as a reredos for the high altar at St George's Chapel, Windsor, took ten carts, each with eight horses, seventeen days to complete the journey.

The only other means of transportation was by river. John Taylor in *A Discovery by Sea* wrote in the early seventeenth century 'there is not any one Town or City which hath a Navigable River at it, that is poore, nor scarce any that are rich, which want a River with the benefits of Boats'.

Derbyshire's only navigable river apart from the lower Derwent was the River Trent, which formed a vital link between Hull and the Midland counties. The successful use of the river below Nottingham and the inability of road transport to cater adequately for the growing needs of the Midland counties led, during the seventeenth century, to a series of attempts to extend the Trent navigation upstream above Wilden Ferry to Burton, a stretch which was obstructed by a weir at King's Mills, and by shallows at the confluence of the Dove, and also to Derby along the lower Derwent which was obstructed by weirs at Wilne and Borrowash.

In 1638 the King ordered the Corporation of Derby to let a house on Derwentside to Sir Cornelius

One of the reasons for improving the Derwent Navigation was to provide an outlet for lead.

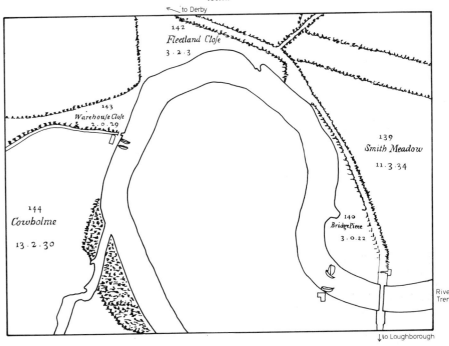

River Trent at Cavendish Bridge (Wilden Ferry) where it is alongside the road. Unloading points marked by boats. Map of 1758.

Vermuyden in order that he could 'make the river of Derwent to be navigable till it fall to Trent'. Houghton in 1693 wrote 'Great endeavours have been made to bring the navigation to Derby, and as far above Darley in the Peak . . .' Seven Bills to improve the Derwent Navigation were presented to Parliament between 1664 and 1719 before assent was eventually given in 1720. The bills were rejected because of opposition from carriers and merchants, boat-owners in the established river ports downstream, local landowners who feared that corn prices might be adversely affected, and from mill-owners, who feared damage to their properties. The improvement to the navigation of the Derwent, which was largely based on George Sorocold's original plans, resulted in the first boat reaching Derby on 17 January 1721 carrying 'Dale-Boards, Tobacco, Fish and other merchandise'. Between June 1728 and June 1729, some 46,052 bushels of grain, malt and beans were brought up the Derwent to Derby. Typical of river navigations in 1789, it was reported to be 'difficult to get a boat up in dry seasons.'

The Trent was navigable to Burton by shallow draught boats in the seventeenth century with the result that in the second half of that century Wilden Ferry, to some extent displaced Nottingham as the head of the Trent navigation. This upper section was controlled by the Fosbrooke family, who leased it from the Cokes of Melbourne along with the control of the ferry-crossing at Wilden.

In 1641 Sir John Coke was asked to supply boats to complete a shipment of 4,000 arms from Hull to West Chester, via Wilden Ferry, for Cromwell's campaign in Ireland and it appears that Fosbrooke supplied the boats to carry the arms from Nottingham to Willington whence they were taken by wagon and packhorse. Cheese from Derby and Ashbourne fairs was one of the significant items of trade according to Lysons. Fosbrooke faced competition from a number of Derby merchants who sent their cheeses downstream from Sawley, so avoiding his transport monopoly. The upshot was that Fosbrooke wrote complaining to Thomas Coke, MP for the Borough of Derby, threatening not to support Coke's future candidature. Fosbrooke's monopoly of the Upper Trent Navigation was partially broken in 1699 by the passing of the Trent Navigation Act. This authorised Sir William Paget to make the river naviagable between Wilden Ferry and Burton upon Trent.

The river lock at King's Mills on the Weston-on-Trent bank of the River Trent.

The control of the upper section of the river above King's Mills was leased from Paget by the Haynes family, whose monopoly Frances Ward of Willington attempted to break.

By 1712 the traffic in cheese, which Defoe estimated at 4,000 tons a year, together with salt from Cheshire and other commodities, had increased beyond all expectations, but regular river navigation was adversely affected by either abnormally wet, dry, or icy conditions. Even so, the Trent was important for the import of hemp and flax from the Baltic countries, timber, potash, foreign

linen, and London groceries including wines, fruits and spices, and flints, the latter carried from southeastern England to Willington, whence they were taken by packhorse to the Potteries. Goods carried downstream included pottery, butter and cheese, salt, hardware, including knives and scythes, lead, millstones, and ale from the various breweries at Burton.

These items were carried in flat-bottomed boats with a capacity of between ten and twenty tons, which had a single sail and were hauled by gangs of men known as halers. The

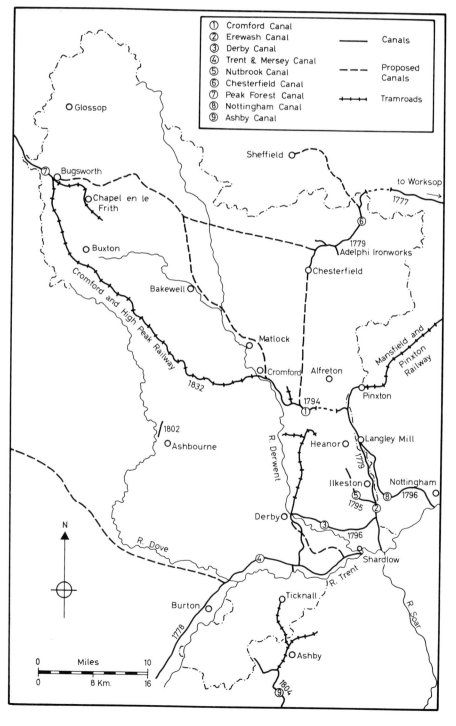

Warehouses alongside the Trent and Mersey Canal at Shardlow with the Trent Brewery chimney (1790). The population grew from 580 (1801) to 750 (1811) to its peak 1,306 (1841).

journey from Burton to Gainsborough and back was achieved in twelve days, including loading and unloading. Later improvements to the navigation of the Trent, by building cuts round the rapids, as at Sawley, did not take place until after the main canals had been constructed. Horses replaced men after 1772, the vicar of Weston-on-Trent remarking on the anticipated unemployment in the village.

In the north-east of the County, goods were transported by packhorse or wagon to Bawtry where they were transferred to 'hoys, lighters, barges or flat-bottomed vessels' (Defoe) on the River Ible. Pilkington calculated that between 1758 and 1783 the total value of lead passing through Bawtry was £105,986. According to Bray (writing in 1777) some lead was sent to Hull via the Rother and Don navigations.

In 1769, James Brindley, born in 1716 at Wormhill near Buxton, and who had served an apprenticeship as a millwright, surveyed the line of the Chesterfield Canal. This was promoted by the London Lead Company as a more efficient method of moving lead from their smelt-mill at Ashover to the river at Bawtry and thence to

Hull; by the Cavendishes who required transport for their Staveley furnace and forge products, and by the North-east Derbyshire coal-owners. Several routes were surveyed, but ultimately Brindley's plans was adopted and the Act for the Chesterfield Canal received the Royal Assent on 28 March 1771. Brindley died before the canal was partly opened on 9 May 1774, following problems in late 1773 in the construction of the 2,850 yard (2,606 metres) Norwood tunnel. As a result of the delay, the whole line of the canal was not opened until 4 June 1777. One immediate result of the opening was that the price of coal at East Retford dropped from 15s 6d (77½p) to 10s 6d (52½p) a ton.

There were several branch canals linking with the Chesterfield Canal, including the Adelphi which linked the ironworks of J. & E. Smith and Co at Duckmanton. Tramways joined collieries, quarries and works with the canal and the goods carried included coal, stone, lead, iron, corn, lime and timber. The canal company paid dividends of between five per cent and eight per cent up to 1836. Various schemes were put forward to link the canal with Sheffield, Derby

and the North West but none were completed because of the difficult intervening terrain.

The Royal Assent for the Trent and Mersey Canal, the Grand Trunk, was given on 14 May 1766, and the whole line of the canal from Derwent Mouth to Preston Brook was opened in 1777, following problems with the Harecastle tunnel. Brindley surveyed the line of the canal as his diary for 1758 shows: 'surveying the novocion (navigation) from Longbrigg (Longbridge, Staffordshire), to King's Mills 12 days ½'. Among this canal's promotors were Josiah Wedgwood and his Scropton-born commercial partner, Thomas Bentley. But Brindley's health caused concern to the promotors and Wedgwood wrote to Bentley in 1767 'I am afraid he will do too much and leave us before his vast designs are executed . . .' Brindley died on 27 September 1772 and Hugh Henshall, his brother-in-law, took over as engineer. The eastern section of the canal was opened as far as Stone on 12 November 1771, but in that year friction between farmers and the Canal Company resulted in Weston Lock being put out of action by 'wanton damage'. Doubts as to the viability of the canal were raised in the *Derby Mercury* on 5 July

1771, which stated: 'Many of the most experienced Navigators and Traders in this County are of the opinion that there is no probability of the Trent and Mersey paying interest'. Ten years later the Company paid a dividend of five per cent and in 1825 £100 shares were worth £2,300.

In 1777 Matthew Pickford, the founder of the famous carrying company, acquired the business of William Bass, who changed from carrying goods between Manchester and London by way of Derby and Ashbourne, to brewing ale at Burton. Pickford, along with other carriers, like the Suttons and Soresbys of Shardlow, the Wheatcrofts of Cromford and Gabriel Brittain of Butterley, ran large fleets of fly-boats and narrow boats on the canals.

To cater for expanding trade, wharves and warehouses were built, and the canal port of Shardlow was developed alongside the Loughborough-Derby turnpike, during the period between 1778 and 1820, as an East Midland equivalent to Stourport. The Derby Canal's link between the Trent and Mersey Canal and the River Trent at Swarkestone was made in 1796, a year after the opening of the Derby Canal itself, which was reported in the *Derby Mercury* of 13 May 1795:

'On Monday 11 May last the Denby line of the Derby Canal and Railway was opened for the conveyance of coal, etc and about 2 o'clock the same day the first boat laden with between 40 and 50 tons of that useful article arrived in this town from the pits at Denby, belonging to William Drury Lowe of Locko, who generously ordered them to be given to the poor and on Tuesday they were distributed accordingly.'

The coal was landed at a wharf near St Mary's Bridge belonging to a Mr Bingham. Farey refers to a boat which carried villagers at 6d (2½p) between Swarkestone and Derby on market days. This was run by Messrs Henshaw and Storer of Weston-on-Trent after 1810. Passenger boats were also run by the Wheatcrofts between Nottingham and Cromford from 1810.

The Erewash Canal, which was surveyed by John Smith in 1776 for the coal masters of the area, received

The Derby Canal Basin, now the site of the Cock Pitt car park. The building on the right was Gandy's warehouse (cheese).

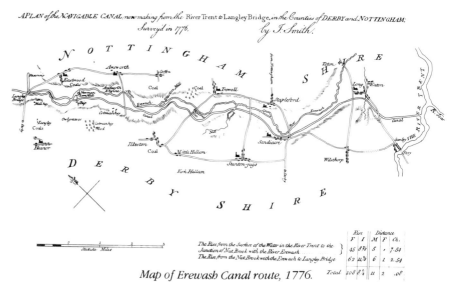

Map of Erewash Canal route, 1776.

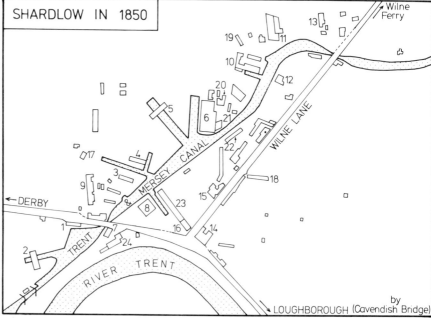

1. 'A' Warehouse.
2. 'B' (Clock) Warehouse
3. 'C' Warehouse
4. 'D' Warehouse
5. 'E' Warehouse
6. Iron Warehouse
7. Salt Warehouse
8. Salt Warehouse.

9. Iron Warehouse.
10. Dockyard and Warehouse
11. Malthouse
12. Trent Brewery
13. New Inn & Shop
14. Navigation Inn & Butcher's Shop
15. Soresby's residence
16. James Clifford's residence

17. William Herod's residence
18. Ropewalk
19. Baptist chapel
20. House (later Ship Inn)
21. Soresby's Wharf & Offices.
22. Stables for canal horses.
23. Sutton's Wharf & Offices.
24. River warehouses.

Bugsworth Canal basin before reclamation. The tramway came from the direction of the pylon and the kilns were to the left of the foreground.

the Royal Assent on 30 April 1777, and work commenced, with John Varley appointed to supervise its construction, at a salary of £220 per annum. The first tolls were collected on the lower section of the canal on 24 October 1778, and the canal was opened throughout in December 1779, following problems with water levels at the upper end. The Canal company was exempted from paying rates and taxes and this was to prove an embarrassment to Long Eaton parish in the 1880s. The Parish took the Company to Court to reverse this state of affairs. Coal, stone and iron goods made up the traffic on the Erewash Canal which was mainly southwards into Leicestershire and Northamptonshire, grain being the principal return cargo.

The catchment area of the Erewash Canal was extended northward with the construction of the Cromford Canal, promoted by Arkwright, and the Gell and Beresford families, the Outrams and the Hodgkinsons. It was engineered by William Jessop of the Butterley Company and was opened in August 1794. Two branch canals were built, one to Pinxton and the other to Lea. The latter was opened in 1802 to serve Peter Night-

ingale's, (later Smedley's), cotton mill. The Cromford Canal passed through the Butterley Tunnel, which restricted the passage of boats to one-way traffic at certain periods of the day. In 1889, subsidence closed the tunnel and, although reopened in 1893, it was closed again in 1900 — although there is oral evidence to indicate the tunnel was used after that date.

The Nutbrook Canal, engineered by Outram, was opened in 1795 specifically to carry coal produced at Sir Henry Hunloke's West Hallam Collieries, although at the time he was in financial difficulty, and those of Edward Miller Mundy at Shipley, but its period of operation was curtailed by subsidence and the limited nature of the traffic. In the north-west of the County, the Peak Forest Canal received the Royal Assent on 28 March 1794 and was in use by 1799 although the flight of locks at Marple was not completed until 1804. Between 1796 and 1804 a tramway was used to by-pass this point. The engineer of the canal was Benjamin Outram of the Butterley Company, and contrary to popular belief, Samuel Oldnow was not the chief promoter, although he became

actively involved following his election in 1794 to the committee for managing the affairs of the Company. The original intention of the canal was to develop the limestone in the north-west of the County, and to supply lime to the agricultural areas of Derbyshire, Lancashire and Cheshire, and gritstone from the Chinley area to the developing industrial towns. The southern end of the canal was at Bugsworth, where there was a large basin with lime kilns supplied by a network of tramways. In the 1880s, approximately 600 tons of lime and limestone were daily shipped out of Bugsworth by thirty to forty narrow boats, although freeze-ups held up the boats in the winter months.

Today the canals are of no economic value except in providing water for agriculture. As a result sections of them have been infilled and made into walkways. Those that are open are being used more and more by pleasure craft and sections of the Erewash and Peak Forest canals have been reopened to meet this increasing demand.

The area served by the canals were extended by tramroads. The terrain south of Bugsworth was too difficult for canal construction but, by building tramways, which were cheaper to construct than canals at about £1,000 per mile, the area serviced by the Peak Forest Canal was extended to Chapel-en-le-Frith, and to Dove Holes by means of inclines and the Chapel Milton tunnel. The cast iron-plate rails for this tramway were supplied by Benjamin Outram and Company at Butterley. Outram was anxious to establish a standard gauge for the tramways, and he wrote to the Ashby de la Zouch Canal Company on 3 December 1799:

'The contractor's estimates and specifications are founded on a design to make the Railways for the carriages of the same width as those of Derby and Crich which are very properly widths for limestone wagons. But as it is exceedingly probable that Railways will soon become general for the transport of merchandise through the commercial parts of this Kingdom and as it appears that many Hogsheads and packages require Carriages eight inches wider than those used on the Railways at Derby and Crich and that carriages fitted for Railways 4'2" in width between the flanches would be wide enough for all sort of loading it seems therefore desirable that all extensive Railways should be of the same width and that width should be sufficient to suit all the purposes of Trade.'

The tramways linked the Ashby Canal with the Ticknall lime quarries in 1803, the Granville Colliery and pottery at Woodville, and Wilkes's coalpit near Measham. It was Joseph Wilkes of Measham who, on 15 August 1799, took a group of people to his Brinsley Colliery in Nottinghamshire to witness a horse pull twenty-one wagons of five-hundred weight each down a 1-in-108 incline on a tramway laid down by Outram; it pulled seven tons up the tramway. Outram also built a tramway which continued the Derby Canal northward from Little Eaton to Smithy Houses, Denby, linking up with several collieries and the Bourne potteries. This horse-drawn railway, which used detachable container wagons, first suggested in 1801, continued operating until 1908. The Crich tramway linked Hilts Quarry at Crich with the Cromford Canal at

The wharf at Little Eaton (1908) where the wagon body was lowered into the canal boat on the Denby line of the Derby Canal.

Bull Bridge where there were lime kilns.

It was on the Fritchley line that Brunton's patent steam propellor which propelled itself forward by means of stilts and which was built at the Butterley Ironworks, where Brunton was the engineer, was tried out in November 1813. A similar machine was built for the Newbottle colliery railway near Durham, but the boiler exploded in 1815. A replacement boiler was lost at sea, but a further one was sent to the colliery. Although it operated for a time, the engine was not a success. Many other tramways were built to complement the Cromford Canal, particularly in the Codnor, Selston and Pinxton area. The Pinxton arm of the canal was eventually linked by an edge-railway, with Bulls Head Lane in Mansfield in 1819, for the specific purpose of supplying that town with coals from the Butterley pits near Pinxton.

Both the Erewash and Nutbrook Canals had tramway links with the many collieries adjoining the two valleys. One of the earliest tramways to be built in Derbyshire was constructed by Joseph Butler in 1788 at Wingerworth, to link his iron furnaces with the iron pits at Woodthorpe End. Butler also built a line from Ankerbold to Lings Colliery, while shortly afterwards, in 1790, the tramway linking Belper with the Mold's Morley Park ironworks was opened.

The Cromford and High Peak

Railway (which received the Royal Assent on 2 May 1825) was originally projected as a canal to link the Cromford and Peak Forest canals across the waterless limestone Peak. It was Josias Jessop, son of William Jessop, who engineered the line, using fish-bellied edge rails, and the first section opened between Cromford Wharf and Hurdlow on 29 May 1830. The line was opened throughout to Whaley Bridge in 1857, linking up with the Peak Forest canal basin. Steam winding engines were used on the three inclines and horses were used on the level, but after 1841 these were replaced by steam locomotives. Passengers, who had to walk up and down the inclines, were carried between 1833 and 1877, in which year the service was terminated following a fatal accident, although in its later days one could ride in the guard's van. At one time the C & HP Railway was seen as one of the key links in the route between London and Manchester. Edward Bradbury described a journey on the railway in 1884, in which he referred to the locomotive working tender first, pulling twenty wagons containing grain, barrels of beer, bags of beans, sewing machines, flour, lime, coal, cans of paint, boxes of tea and agricultural implements. In its later years it was important during the summer months for taking water to villages on the dry limestone upland. Today the line is closed and used as a walkway.

The building of the canals, tramways and later the railways required

Fish-bellied rails, produced by the Butterley Company for the Cromford and High Peak Railway, in the engine shed at High Peak Junction.

High Peak Junction. The junction of the Cromford and High Peak Railway with the Cromford Canal.

Nottingham and Derby. This route was surveyed by William Jessop and approved by George Rennie, but two attempts to place a Bill before Parliament in 1833 and 1834 failed through insufficient financial backing. Lancashire supporters of the scheme demanded a re-survey of the route and as a result Charles B.Vignoles was appointed engineer to the Midland Counties Railway in 1835.

Amended plans were passed through Parliament in 1836 but, because of opposition from the North Midland Railway Company and the various canal companies, in the House of Lords, and because there was no major town, the Erewash Valley section of the original scheme was abandoned. The Derby-Nottingham and Long Eaton-Rugby lines were sanctioned on 21 June 1836 and the first sod was cut in May 1838, the Derby-Nottingham line being opened to the public on 4 June 1839 using a temporary platform at Derby with trains drawn by engines built at the Butterley works, although these were not very successful. The Long Eaton-Rugby section was opened the following year, and this line connected with the Birmingham-London Railway. The passenger carrying side of the Midland Counties' operation, like that of the Liverpool-Manchester railway, was initially more lucrative than freight carriage.

Two other Derbyshire railways were sanctioned in the same session of Parliament. On 19 May 1836, the Bill for the Birmingham-Derby Junction line was passed, followed two months later by the Act for the North Midland line. George Stephenson was appointed as engineer for both of these lines, but eventually George's thirty-four-year-old son Robert took over completion of the Birmingham and Derby Junction line. This was opened to public traffic on 12 August 1839, thereby giving Derby further access to London by rail. The duplication was referred to in the *Athenaeum* in 1843; 'When going north (from London), we have two lines parallel with each other, the Birmingham and Derby, and the Midland Counties, the latter of which should never have existed — total loss

miles of stone-walling, fences and quickthorn hedges. One of the main sources of the quicksets was Melbourne. In 1826 the Ashby Canal Company ordered the purchase of between forty and fifty-thousand quicksets, costing 5s 0d (25p) per thousand, for the fencing of their tramways.

Although there were many horse-drawn tramways in the County, it was not until 1839 that locomotive-hauled passenger carrying railways were inaugurated into Derby. The coming of the railway marked a watershed in Derby's history, changing it from a rather sleepy market town with a few locally-based industries, to a thriving industrial centre

in the second half of the nineteenth century. The railway had much the same effect on Chesterfield after 1840, as well as opening up other fairly inaccessible places, particularly between Sheffield and Manchester.

The coalowners of the Erewash Valley, realising that they were losing the valuable Leicester market following the opening of the Leicester to Swannington Railway in 1832, asked the canal companies to reduce their charges to meet the competition of Leicestershire coal. When the reduction eventually materialised it was too late. The owners met at the Sun Inn at Eastwood on 16 August 1832 and agreed to build a railway from Pinxton to Leicester, with links to

The North Midland line at Bull Bridge.

Thompson's Derby Station.

Each railway company had its engine sheds and workshops at Derby. In the middle distance are the North Midland houses, and behind them Bemrose's printing works.

£1,000,000'. The three companies, under the guidance of the Borough Council, eventually agreed to build a joint station on the Holmes at Derby, the architect being Francis Thompson of the North Midland. Wishaw described the stations on the North Midland line as affording 'the architect ample scope for the exercise of his talent which is strikingly exhibited throughout the whole of the permanent buildings of this railway. But...we cannot but deplore the growing evil of expending large sums of money on railway appendages. Instead of cottage buildings which . . .would have been amply sufficient, we find the railway liter-

ally ornamented with so many beautiful villas . . .'

The station at Derby, which was described as a 'market-place for steam engines', was opened on 11 May 1840, the day that the North Midland line between Derby and Masborough was opened to the public, but the idea of a single long platform with bays for the three companies was not carried through. Alongside the station were built the round houses for the maintenance of engines and carriages of each of the Companies. The work force that came to Derby with the development of the railway complex was housed in the Litchurch area, on land which had belonged to

the Borough family. It was the North Midland Railway which provided the first houses, as well as a public house, in Railway Terrace in the 1840s. Soon after this, Derby almost had a fourth railway. A line from Derby to Manchester via Ashbourne was proposed, but opposition from landowners caused the scheme to be abandoned. Fierce competition for traffic resulted in all three companies losing money, and in the case of the North Midland, under George Hudson's guidance, lowering standards of safety. The only solution was an amalgamation, and this took place on 10 May 1844, when the Midland Railway Company was formed under the chairmanship of George Hudson, with its headquarters at Derby.

In the following year the Midland Railway took over the Leicester-Swannington Railway and extended it to Burton upon Trent, and in 1846 the Ashby Canal was absorbed, along with its tramways. The Erewash Valley line at Pinxton, originally promoted in the Midland Counties Railway Bill was eventually opened on 6 September 1847, and was later extended northwards to join up with the old North Midland line near Clay Cross in 1862. The Midland Railway did not have a London terminal station and in its early years was forced to use Euston. On 1 February 1858, following a link-up with the Great Northern Railway, the Midland Railway was able to run into King's Cross Station, but inevitably MR trains had to take second place to those of the GNR.

In 1862 it was claimed that no fewer than 3,400 Midland Railway trains had been delayed and this led in 1863 to the MR obtaining an act to build a new line from Bedford to its proposed new London terminus — St Pancras. The ironwork for the roof of St Pancras was constructed by the Butterley Company, whose engineer-in-chief, William Henry Barlow, was advised by Rowland Mason Ordish, who was born at Melbourne and who designed the Royal Albert Bridge over the Thames. St Pancras was opened to Midland Railway passenger traffic on 1 October 1868, and was the last of the major London stations to be built.

The line from Derby north to Manchester posed severe engineering problems. After various attempts by the Midland Railway, in association with other railway companies, to bring into existence a line between Derby and Manchester, it was the Manchester, Buxton, Matlock, and Midland Junction Railway which eventually built the eleven miles of track from Ambergate to Rowsley which were opened on 4 June 1849. A terminal station, designed by Paxton of Crystal Palace fame, was built at Rowsley for travellers to and from Chatsworth. It had been proposed to continue this line northward through Chatsworth Park, but the Duke of Devonshire, like the Duke

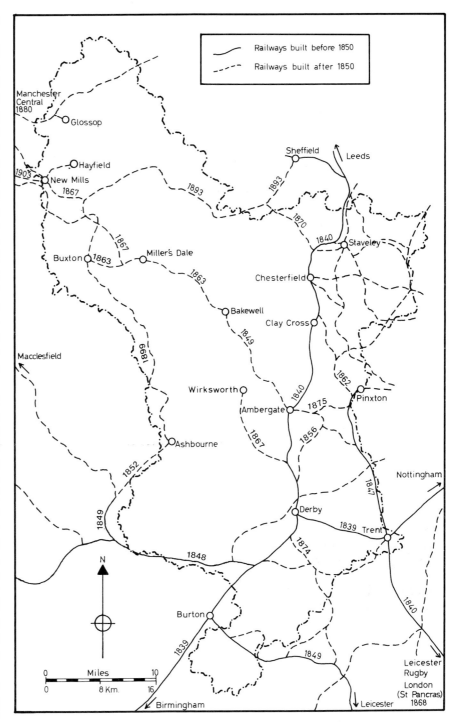

of Rutland, was opposed to railways passing over his land and particularly in sight of his house. The MR planned an alternative route through Duffield to Wirksworth, which was opened in 1867, and which it intended to extend to Rowsley in case it did not receive running rights on the Ambergate-Rowsley section.

The Act for a line from Rowsley to Buxton was passed on 25 May 1860. This followed the Wye Valley through a cut and cover tunnel in the grounds of Haddon Hall and was opened on 1 June 1863. At this time

the LNWR came to an arrangement with the Great Northern and the Manchester, Sheffield and Lincolnshire Railway, to build a line from Whaley Bridge to Buxton — the reason for Buxton's twin stations. The final link between Derby and Manchester was made when the Midland Railway came to an arrangement with the Manchester, Sheffield and Lincolnshire Railway Company to build a line from Buxton to New Mills and to use the latter's track into London Road Station in Manchester. The railway

Osmaston Hall (1802), bought by the Midland Railway to extend its carriage and wagon works. Demolished in 1938.

Friar Gate. Great Northern Railway bridge built by Handysides. Immediately to the left were the horse-tram stables.

Construction work on the LNW line to Buxton, to the north of Ashbourne (1897/8).

Ashbourne Station (1852/3) replaced by a wooden LNWR station in 1899.

'Hummy' at Stretton, en route Ashover to Clay Cross.

Ashover local bus operator (1939) to Chesterfield and Alfreton.

had finally broken through, and that saw the end of the stage-coach.

For the Midland Railway, the joint line to Manchester posed similar disadvantages to the London access, chiefly because it belonged to a company competing for the all-important Manchester-London traffic. So the Midland Railway built a link from Gowholes Junction to the Cheshire Lines Company at Throstle Nest Junction and ran into Manchester Central Station. This terminus, which was never fully completed, was built in 1880 with a roof similar to that of St Pancras, by Andrew Handyside and Company of Derby. The first trains ran into Manchester Central on 1 July 1880.

Chesterfield was linked with Sheffield on 2 February 1870, so forming an important Midland Railway junction. The Manchester, Sheffield and Lincolnshire Railway Company eventually opened a line linking Chesterfield with Annesley (2 January 1893), the line to Nottingham being completed in 1898 (the Great Central). A third railway company, the Lancashire, Derbyshire and East Coast Railway, linked Chesterfield with the city of Lincoln, on 8 March 1897.

The Midland Railway was one of the more progressive companies, using the first steel rail in 1857, converting engines from coke-to-coal-burning between 1856 and 1860, and in 1872 announcing that it would put on Third Class coaches with padded seats on all trains, leading to the abolition of Second Class travel in 1875.

The first excursion train to be run by an indivdual was organised by the evangelist Thomas Cook of Melbourne on 5 July 1841 in conjunction with the Midland Counties Railway Company, from Leicester to Loughborough at a shilling (5p) a head. It was Cook, the originator of the travel firm, who persuaded the Dukes of Rutland and Devonshire to open their estates to public excursions in 1848. Excursions had been run by the railway companies almost from their inception. The North Midland Railway ran one from Sheffield to the Derby Arboretum soon after its opening in 1840.

In 1888 the Midland Railway Company acquired Osmaston Hall, which had been built in 1696, along with the Wilmot's estate, for extensions to their Carriage and Wagon Works. This was one of several country houses and estates to be absorbed into the expanding boundaries of the Borough of Derby in the nineteenth and twentieth centuries.

In 1923 the Midland Railway was amalgamated with other companies to form the London, Midland and Scottish Railway Company. Following the nationalisation of the railways in 1947, Derby Locomotive Works became one of the major centres for the development, construction and maintenance of diesel locomotives in the London Midland Region of British Railways, the last steam locomotive being constructed in the Derby works in June 1957.

Two other main lines ran into Derby. The North Staffordshire Railway was opened between Derby and Crewe on 9 October 1848, and thirty years later the Great Northern

Railway, which ran into Friar Gate Station, was operating between Nottingham and Derby. This line was extended to Eggington Junction in 1880. The GNR line was built to draw some of the lucrative Erewash Valley coal traffic from the Midland Railway.

Ashbourne was not linked by rail until 31 March 1852, when the opening of the line to Uttoxeter was celebrated with 'feasting, dancing, church bells, the choir of the Collegiate Church of Manchester rendering "Hail Smiling Morn" and other suitable works and innumerable speeches of mutual congratulation'. A banquet for 350 people was held in what was to become the goods warehouse, as the passenger station had not yet been built. The workers, 420 in all, were entertained in a marquee 'at a discreet distance away'. The original station was replaced by a wooden one, typical of those built by the LNWR, when the line was extended to Buxton in the 1890s, being completed in 1899. This particular line was important in the 1900s for its daily milk train to London and a through train to Euston. Swadlincote, in the south of the County, was linked by rail in 1851, when a branch was built to join the Burton to Leicester line.

Between 1929 and 1940, passengers were carried between Ashover and Clay Cross on the Ashover Light Railway, a line using equipment from the War Stores Disposals Board and constructed by the Clay Cross Company, primarily to transport limestone from its quarries at Ashover and Milltown.

The main A6 route through Derby, pictured in the late 1930s.

An interesting aspect of the Midland Railway's activities was the construction of the 3ft 6in gauge light railway which ran on roads and through fields between Burton and Ashby from July 1900 to February 1927, serving Newhall and Swadlincote.

Today none of the tramways and light railways exist, and although Derby has rail links with Nottingham, Stoke, Sheffield and Manchester, Matlock and London, it is no longer the nodal point of the rail network of the Midlands that it was in the nineteenth and the first half of the twentieth century. Nor does Trent Station exist.

There had been a horse-drawn street tramway in Derby since 1880, the horses stabled on Midland Road and under the viaduct arches of the Great Northern Railway near Friar Gate Station, and this supplemented the horse buses which Wallace Wallis had commenced running from the station to the Market Place in 1840. The Derby municipal tramway system was completely electrified in 1909 and ran until 1933, when trolley-buses replaced the trams, having been introduced in 1932.

Work on a street tramway in Ilkeston commenced on 1 November 1901, operating from 1903 to 1931,

Opening day of the Ilkeston tramway system, 16 May 1903.

drawing from the Nottinghamshire and Derbyshire Electric Power Company's power plant at Manner's Colliery in Ilkeston. The Electric Power Company later built the Spondon Power Station to supply the towns of the Lower Erewash Valley.

At one time it was proposed that there should be a comprehensive tramway system linking Nottingham, Heanor, Ripley, Alfreton, Belper, Ilkeston, Long Eaton, Bees-

ton and Derby, but problems of gauge, opposition to the Derby and Nottingham Light Railway Company's plans by the railway companies, and the problem of the level crossing in Nottingham Road, Long Eaton, reduced this to only one route, from Nottingham to Ripley, opened on 1 January 1914. This lengthy country route, the 'Ripley Rattler', was converted to trolley buses on 5 October 1933 and continued running

Photographed in 1920 on Whatstandwell Bridge, this Trent bus operated until 1933.

A Barton bus turning from College Street into Derby Road, Long Eaton, in 1926.

Trent and two of the competition in Ilkeston Market Place, pictured in 1926. Town Hall opened 1868 for the Local Government Board (1864).

until 1953. Both Glossop and Chesterfield were also served by tramway systems, the latter having horse trams in 1882 with electrification after 1904 and trolley buses in 1927. Matlock had a cable tramway between 1893 and 1927, a venture which was initially supported by the MP, George Newnes, a native of the town. This tramway transported passengers up Matlock Bank to the hydros.

Derby was the headquarters of the Trent Motor Traction Company which is today part of the National Bus Company. Trent began their operations in 1913 as Commercial Car Hirers who supplied a Scottish landowner with transport for his shooting parties. One of the guests was the owner of Osmaston Manor, near Ashbourne, and it was he who decided the vehicle would be ideal for transporting staff and guests from Ashbourne to Derby. So began a regular service between the two places, with the buses garaged at the Green Man Hotel in Ashbourne. Instead of a London headquarters, it was decided to form a local company, under the chairmanship of Alderman W.Hart, a former Mayor. Merging with the bus interests of the British Electric Traction Company Limited, the promoters formed the Trent Motor Traction Company Limited, registered on 31 October 1913, with services from Derby to Ashbourne and to Alfreton, and between Alfreton and Chesterfield, with buses in a green livery. A year later services were introduced to Melbourne and to Burton, all 'buses departing from outside the Corn Exchange in Derby.

Thomas Henry Barton ran a public service in the Little Eaton and Derby area in 1898, while assisting in his family's quarrying activities, and on 6 October 1908 started a Long Eaton to Nottingham service. It was the beginnings of a thriving bus operation which absorbed many of the small companies operating in the Erewash Valley.

Following World War One, many small operators emerged, adapting war surplus vehicles for the transport of passengers on market days, thus taking over the village carrier's function. Webster of Hognaston, a bus operator, was the village carrier, as between the wars were the Fox

R101 flying over Ilkeston in 1929. Stanton Ironworks had been bombed by a Zeppellin during World War One.

Brothers of Woolley, near Ashover. Buses were also used for carrying miners to work, workers and shoppers to Derby and Nottingham as well as for excursions, so competing with the railways. Services evolved on an *ad hoc* basis, with competition developing on the more lucrative runs. As a result, the smaller operators were unable to compete, and gradually they were amalgamated with or absorbed by the bigger companies; for example, Trent ran Harrison's Ashbourne service off the road in 1915, took over the Loughborough Road Car Company in 1919 and Higgs and Waller of Melbourne in 1929, along with many others.

In 1929 the Midland General Omnibus Company Limited, which had commenced operating in 1922 and later merged with Trent Motor Traction in 1972, took over Williamson's Garage Limited of Heanor, although the latter had a larger fleet of buses. The competition for passengers continued, at risk to life and limb, until the Road Traffic Act of 1930 formalised the licensing of routes, which had previously had to be negotiated with each local authority through which the service tra-

The Cat and Fiddle was a popular destination, particularly in the early days of the motorcar. The 'British' omnibus is on the Macclesfield-Buxton service. This photograph was taken in the late 1920s.

velled, and for each bus and driver operating on the route. The Act also imposed certain mechanical constraints so that by 1933 most of the small operators had disappeared. It is interesting to note that with the contraction of services and the amalgamation of the major bus companies, small bus operators are once again flourishing, providing private hire, and town and country services.

The first aeroplane to be seen in Derby was a Bleriot which landed on

the Racecourse on 11 July 1912. Seventeen years later, a year before it crashed, the R101 airship flew over Derby and Ilkeston. In June 1939, Derby Municipal Airport at Burnaston was opened and East Midlands Airport was opened, for daylight flights only, in April 1965 and Burnaston continued for pleasure flying as the base for Derby Aero Club until it was moved in 1990 to make way for the Toyota car factory.

Townscape

THERE were only two settlements in the County which could be termed urban in the pre-industrial period: Derby, the County town, and Chesterfield. The Romans established a ford at Little Chester to guard the fort where Rykneld Street crossed the River Derwent, with a Romano-British settlement outside the fort area. The Saxons established their community at the junction of the Markeaton and Bottle Brooks, some way from the Roman camp. The Saxon vill was named *Northweorthig* (Northworthy) and was centred on the site of St Werburgh's Church, some time towards the end of the seventh century. The churchyard became the 'Cheap' or Market Place. Some time about AD 875, the Danes captured Northworthy and, in dismembering the Kingdom of Mercia, established their settlement of *Deoraby* on the site of the present Market Place, near the confluence of the Markeaton Brook and the River Derwent. Derby was one of five Royal Boroughs of the Danelaw in the time of Canute, and was an established military base, and a trading centre with its own mint.

The re-introduction of Christianity when the Saxons recaptured the town resulted in the building of several churches including St Alkmund's. It is possible that a castle was built by the Danes on Castle Fields, the approach to it from the west following a route closely approximating to East Street, previously called Bag Lane, and which in a deed dated 1647 was referred to as Castle Gate.

Little is known of the town until the Norman Conquest. From the Domesday Book we learn that, in the time of Edward the Confessor, that is before the Conquest, the town had 243 burgesses (forty-one of whom had twenty-four carucates [ploughland] of taxable land), six churches and fourteen watermills, most of these being fulling mills. Two-thirds of the annual revenue from the town went to the King and one-third to the Earl of Mercia in whose Earldom it lay.

However, by the time the Domesday Survey was compiled there had been a decline in the number of burgesses to 141 (Nottingham had 136 burgesses) and ten mills, while 103 houses stood desolate. From then on dues which had been paid to the King were conferred on William Peverel. The neighbouring manor of Ludecerce (Litchurch) appears to have been added to the Borough about then but retained its identity, and it seems likely that following the Conquest, the Normans established the nearby settlement of Normanton.

Shortly after the Conquest, the church of St James was given to the Cluniac monks of Bermondsey, and this gift was confirmed by Stephen in 1140, when the monks established a priory whence they fostered town trade by establishing the annual fair of St James. Three other religious houses were closely connected with the early history of Derby; the Augustinian Abbey of St Mary at Darley founded in 1137, the Benedictine Nunnery of St Mary de Pratis established in 1160, and the Dominican Friary set up between 1224 and 1238.

The origin of the liberties and privileges of the Borough go back to a charter granted in 1155 by Henry I, which gave the burgesses, who were a self-electing body, the right to hold a market and fair. Henry II confirmed these privileges, and in a further charter granted by John in 1204, the Borough gained even more self-government than it had previously possessed, the burgesses being authorised to appoint annually at the Feast of St Michael, a Bailiff whose duty it was to collect the King's dues.

The office of Reeve had previously been the appointee of the King, and was frequently an outsider who resorted to oppressive measures to achieve his ends. Other privileges held by the burgesses included the monopoly of cloth-dyeing and fulling within a radius of ten miles around Derby, although Nottingham controlled the wool trade, rights of toll in connection with trade, and the punishment of thieves in the County area adjacent to the Borough, this conflicting with the authority of the Lords of the adjacent Manors who dispensed justice through the Manorial Courts. For these privileges, the burgesses had to pay sixty-six marks and two palfreys, small saddle horses.

The burgesses also paid ten marks for the privilege of expelling the colony of Jews, who had settled outside the town in the area indicated today by Jury (Jewry) Street. The Charter also confirmed the right to hold fairs and markets, and the present Market Place was created some time between 1285 and 1308, following the Act which prohibited fairs being held in churchyards. In 1290 Edward I granted his share of the town's revenue for four years for the purpose of paying for the Market Square. Burgesses were also given the right to form a Gild Merchant, this demonstrating that the trade of the town was substantial. The Gild allowed its members to trade freely and required all those who worked at one trade to live in the same locality, hence the names Iron Gate, Sadler Gate, and Full Street. This resulted in each trade establishing its Craft Gild, restricting Gild privileges to as small a number of persons as possible, out of the total population at this time of approximately 3,000. In 1330 the Gild Merchant was accused of acting oppressively, permitting visiting merchants to sell their fares wholesale and only to members of the Gild. Naturally they could fix their own price by forming a ring and the result was that the Gild was convicted of unjust practices and fined forty marks.

Trade developed during the thirteenth and fourteenth centuries, the chief items being wine, wool, sheepskins, leather and lead, but river access was impeded in the thirteenth century by the Abbot of Dale building weirs at Borrowash for his corn mills.

In 1295 Derby sent two representatives to the twenty-third Parliament of Edward I, the first Borough Members being John de la Cornere and Ranulph de Makeneye. About 1330, St Mary's bridge was rebuilt in stone and the bridge chapel erected. Plague and pestilence were common throughout the period. During the Black Death, which reached the County in May 1349, the Prior of the Friary, the Prioress of the Nunnery and the chantry priest of St Peter's died along with a significant number of the town's population. For those suffering from leprosy a leper hospital was built outside the town dedicated to St Leonard.

The privileges of the burgesses and the two bailiffs were confirmed in successive Charters by Edward III, Henry VI, Edward IV and Richard III, although the renewal of a charter could not be taken for granted. Three years after Edward III had confirmed the privileges granted by King John in 1327, he called upon the burgesses to show by what right they enjoyed their privileges, whereupon 'the Burgesses produced several old Charters, upon which the King on their consenting to pay a fine of 40 markes, restored their liberties'. Judicial

matters in the Borough at this time were dealt with by the burgesses in the 'Moot Hall', which was probably sited between Iron Gate and Full Street.

As a result of an Act of 1536, the smaller monasteries and nunneries were dissolved, and this saw the end of the Nunnery, the Priory and the Friary in Derby. Henry VIII was also responsible for confiscating a large amount of the property which belonged to the Gilds. Following the accession of Queen Mary, the monastic lands which had not been sold off and were still in the possession of the Crown as a result of the dissolution of the monasteries, were given to the Borough. As a result the town area was increased by the inclusion of Nun's Green, Castle Fields and the corn mill at the bottom of St Michael's Lane.

It was during the sixteenth century that several charities were established. A few years before the dissolution, Robert Liversage, a wealthy dyer who traded at the corner of the Corn Market, by a deed dated 21 August 1529, granted property in various parts of the town to the vicar of St Peter's and seven other trustees. The revenue from these properties was to be used for paying a priest to say daily mass for the souls of the donor and his wife, and also to pay every Friday a silver penny to thirteen poor men and women who attended mass. The monies from this charity were used to build almshouses in St Peter's Churchyard in 1722, and on London Road and Nottingham Road between 1836 and 1878. Bess of Hardwick, in a letter dated 3 March 1597, proposed to build two almshouses, one at Bakewell and the other in Full Street, Derby. Bess laid down a strict regime for the seven brothers and four sisters who occupied the Derby almshouses. Twice a day they had to attend prayers, when a creed, collect and a prayer 'for our noble founder . . .and all children' were said, and the penalty for missing the prayers was a fine of two pence.

Bess's prisoner, Mary Queen of Scots, when transferred from South Wingfield to Tutbury, stayed overnight on 13 January 1585 at Babington Hall in the town because, as Sir Ralph Sadler in whose charge she

was, wrote: 'the wayes being so foul and depe . . .we cannot go throughe in a daye'. Three years later, among the list of subscribers to a fund for building ships to repel the Spanish Armada were the names of three Derby tradesmen — William Botham, draper, Richard Fletcher and Edward Smithe, both butchers, who each subscribed the then large sum of £25. In 1592-3, the town was once again visited by the plague, when it was particularly severe on the populace living in the parishes of St Alkmund, and of All Saints, the Vicar of which church wrote: 'there was not two houses together free from ytt'. This was probably a recurrence of cholera, which was endemic throughout the period and into the nineteenth century.

During the sixteenth century there were frequent disputes between the burgesses and the rest of the townfolk, who were referred to as the 'community', over the question of common rights. The town fields were farmed on a communal basis, but when the lands were annually apportioned it was the burgesses who obtained the better plots, which in course of time they enclosed for themselves. In 1495, the 'Bayley and Burgesses' were ordered to throw open Chester Green, an area of common land which they had enclosed, and in 1603-04, three burgesses were committed to jail for damage done in enclosing land. The sale of part of the common pasture of Nun's Green was to be a bone of contention in connection with the Paving and Lighting Act of 1792.

At the beginning of the seventeenth century, there were approximately 4,000 inhabitants in the Borough. On 7 March 1661, nineteen years after Charles I passed through Derby, James I granted the town a new Charter which confirmed the old privileges and granted new ones. From this date the Corporation was to consist of two Bailiffs and twenty-four Burgesses, with a Recorder and a Chamberlain. The Charter prohibited any stranger from carrying on trade in the town except at markets and fairs, but if a stranger was allowed to carry on trade for a year and a day, he became a freeman of the Borough.

Trade at this time was much as

All Saints' Church from St Mary's Gate at the bottom of which were the Courts and the parish corn-mill.

AD 1000
ELIZABETHAN
AFTER SILK MILL
1860
PRESENT BUILT UP AREA

0   Mile   ½
0   Km.   ½

The growth of Derby's built-up area.

William Camden described it. He referred to the 'excellent malt liquor', and went on to say, 'the wealth of the town arises from buying up corn and retailing it to the people of the uplands'. The wool trade had declined but Derby continued to be an important trading centre for lead. In 1693, Houghton listed 694 dwelling houses for a population of 4,164, served by 76 malthouses and 120 alehouses. Derby 'Canary Ale' was much esteemed. Celia Fiennes, who travelled the county on horseback at the end of the seventeenth century, found Derby expensive for provisions and commented on the number of glove-makers, and the use of sledges for transport. She also mentioned the 'remarkable wheel' which had been erected by George Sorocold in 1692 to raise water from the Derwent to a point near St Michael's Church, whence it was supplied to the town-folk by elm pipes laid through 'the

King's Streete, Irongate, Market Place, Rotten Row and the Corne Market in Derby, and some to the Goale Bridge . . .' In 1789, Sorocold's wheel supplied a thousand house-holds at twenty shillings a year and there were 'common cocks for the poor'. Public wells, which were the responsibility of the Corporation, were the other source of water, two being St Alkmund's and Becket Wells.

Henry Mellor was proclaimed the first Mayor of the Borough on 3 July 1637 as a result of the Charter granted in that year by Charles I, which specified that the Corporate Body was to consist of a Mayor, nine Aldermen, fourteen Brethren and fourteen Capital Burgesses. Unfortunately Mellor died before his term of office was completed, and John Hope, who had held the office of second Bailiff in 1637, became Mayor. The Mayor was elected at a meeting of the aldermen,

brothers and capital burgesses which was held in All Saints' Church at Michaelmas. From All Saints' the Corporate Body proceeded to the Market Head to present the newly elected Mayor to their fellow bur-gesses. Among the responsibilities of the Mayor was that of seeing that the standard measures were observed in the Borough and that the 'Assize of Bread' was observed by the bakers. Bakers who broke the law regarding the size of the farthing loaf were punished by means of the 'cucking stool' which was placed over the dam of the corn mill at the bottom of St Mary's Gate.

Miscreants were placed in the town gaol, which had been built in 1568 from monies raised by a new tax, across Markeaton Brook between the Corn Market and St Peter's Street. Anthony Fitzherbert, imprisoned for his religious beliefs, decribed the gaol as 'most odyous for many causes,

The meeting house in St Michael's Lane, where Wesley preached, built 1764/5.

The pre-1863 toll house, Kedleston Road, on the Derby-Brassington turnpike (1738).

The Piazzas at Derby's Market Head, built 1708, and demolished by 1871, was celebrated by a firework display (21 July).

The Strand, Derby, culverted between 1863 and 1877 and pictured here when opened for repair work in 1963.

which the lothsome and unsaverye smells, and the combersome companyons wch be hether remytted for all vyces . . .' This gaol was replaced by one in Friar Gate in 1756, which was a response to the increasing incidence of rioting, particularly regarding the price of bread and cheese. In 1766, the Derby 'crowd' prevented 'boats loaded with cheese from going down the water'. This was the period of the organised mob. In July 1795, Ilkeston colliers left their work and toured the County 'in a disorderly manner' and in August, colliers from Newhall and Swadlincote collieries assembled 'at the sound of a horn' for the purpose of obtaining wheat at a reduced price.

In 1674 the tradesmen of Derby formed themselves into a Company of Mercers 'for the inspection and regulating of trade and commerce in the said Borough and avoiding frauds and deceits in the way of trade . . .' In practice this body revived the worst features of the mediaeval gilds with the Corporation protecting their

interests. Such an abuse of privilege occurred in 1693, when the Mayor and Burgesses granted to five Derby gentlemen the lease of St Michael's Mill, ' . . .with the Piscary of Fishinge of the River Darwent', the agreement continuing 'The Mayor, Aldermen, Brethren and Common Councell have liberty to fish with ye Rod in the Piscary or Fisher', and the Mayor and Chamberlain for the time being may have 'a day of fishing yearly in the said River att a seasonable tyme in the yeare with nettes'.

Twenty-seven years after this, the Derwent was made navigable following a long period of frustrating opposition. In 1702 Sorocold had produced a plan to make the river navigable, which involved the making of four cuts and the building of nine locks to avoid shallows, as well as the mills at Wilne and Borrowash. It was about this time that Derby's newer industries began to develop.

Framework knitting had been one urban occupation during the late

seventeenth century but, following Cotchett's establishment of the silk mill in 1702, trade expanded, and along with the setting up in 1756 of the Cockpit Hill pottery by local banker John Heath, the town prospered. Communications were improved with the introduction of waggon services in the early eighteenth century, and later coach services were developed following the establishment of turnpike trusts.

Between 4 and 6 December 1745 the town was 'host' to Bonnie Prince Charlie and his troops, while nineteen years later Derby was visited by John Wesley for the first time, both events being reported in the *Derby Mercury*. Wesley was shouted down in the Market Place and some disorder followed, but the following year he spoke at a meeting house which had been built next to a fellmonger's yard in St Michael's Lane. The Quakers were already established in the town. It is believed that the term 'Quaker' was first used

Floodwater, a recurrent hazard, in the Cornmarket, Derby, on 22 May 1932 after Markeaton Brook burst its banks.

in the trial at Derby in 1650 of George Fox, who previously had been in Chesterfield.

Towards the end of the eighteenth century, Derby, the population of which had grown to about 10,000, had become the centre of a comprehensive system of turnpike roads, was linked by canal after 1791 to the east and west coasts, had a large source of coal a few miles to the north and east, and was experiencing industrial expansion, particularly in textiles. The first signs of engineering can be found in the establishment of a clock-making business in 1776 by James Whitehurst. From Whitehursts evolved John Smith and Company Limited who made 'Great Tom' for St Paul's, along with other famous clocks. John Davis also made survey instruments.

In 1789, when there was one alehouse to every sixteen inhabitants, it was prohibited to leave in the streets at night such items as butchers' blocks, waggons, carts and post chaises. In the same year the building of a wider toll-free St Mary's Bridge was commenced with monies raised by subscription, largely under the initiative of William Strutt. Three years later an Act was passed authorising the 'paving, cleansing, lighting (of) . . .the streets . . .within the borough of Derby'.

As a result of this, the streets were lit by oil lamps from September to April except for eight days round the full moon. In order to provide the funds for the lighting and paving of the streets, that portion of Nun's Green which still remained the property of the Corporation was sold in 1792. Daniel Parker Coke, the MP for Nottingham, but who lived in Full Street, Derby, fought hard to keep the Green for the public and the pros and cons of the case were put forward in a series of broadsheets.

On 19 February 1821, the Market Place, which was much smaller than it is today because of the Piazzas and the Town Hall, was lit with gas. This was shortly after those judged responsible for the Pentrich Rising had been hanged at the town gaol in Friar Gate, and before the *Derby and Chesterfield Reporter* was established to counter the views expressed by the Tory *Derby Mercury*.

Public hangings attracted large crowds until the last public execution in the town in 1862. Other entertainment was to be found in the fairs held in the Morledge, and the Shrovetide football. A curate from Bath, Revd Richard Warner, visiting the town in 1802 wrote 'it (Derby) was . . .in itself worth seeing, from the beauty of its situation on the Derwent, and the pleasing scenery of its environs'. He referred to six silk mills, and visited Carr's porcelain manufactory as well as Brown and Company's marble works.

Not all was peaceful. When news came of the defeat of the First Reform Bill in 1830 a mourning peal was rung and a mob attacked Bemrose's house in the Market Place. It was reported that Lady Mundy of Markeaton did not undress for four nights for fear of being attacked! The next day the mob attacked the gaol in Friar Gate, which was 'insufficient and insecure as well as wrong or defective in construction', and released the prisoners. At the Vernon Street gaol, built in 1827, the mob were fired on by warders. The Hussars were called out and dispersed the rioters, but not before they had demolished a house in Chester Green.

Following the Reform Act of 1832, 1,384 persons in the Borough became eligible to vote. In December 1833 the town was visited by two Royal Commissioners to enquire into abuses in the Borough's administration, but in spite of evidence to show that much public property had passed into private possession, Commissioner Rushton decided that the town had suffered no loss, as the value of public property was no less than it had been in 1652.

As a result of the Municipal Corporations Act of 1835, the exclusive rights of the burgesses were abolished, and the election of the Town Council was vested in householders who paid £10 a year rent. The town was divided into six wards, each

The North Midland and the Midland Counties Railway metals joined before entering Derby Station, crossing the River Derwent and the Derby Canal. (1840s).

Ockbrook was a sought-after address, particularly after the railway was opened on 4 June 1839.

Derby riverside in the 1850s.

Iron Gate, Derby, before widening in 1864.

of which returned six Councillors, they being elected at an open booth set up for each ward in the Market Place. Following the two extensions of the Borough in 1877 and 1901, the wards were increased to sixteen.

In 1836 a new police force was established comprising eight men; the Borough also employed ten night watchmen, who had to 'clock-in' on a system introduced by William Strutt. There were 210 gas lamps and 110 oil lamps to light the streets. Following the serious flooding in the town centre on 1 April 1842, a large section of Markeaton Brook was culverted. Fifty years previously, the Corporation, with the help of public subscriptions, had renewed several of the bridges that took the town's streets across the brook. Sadler Gate and St Peter's bridges each cost over £500 to rebuild in 1789/90.

Although the canal to Derby resulted in industrial development in the area of Cockpit Hill and the Morledge, as well as on land near where the canal joined the river by St Mary's Bridge, it was the railways

which in 1839 and 1840 gave real impetus to industry, particularly engineering. In the Derby Mercury of October 1835 it was suggested that railways 'would make Derby a centre of communication and must, we imagine, increase the trade and importance of the town'. This was to be proved correct. For a few months, Derby businessmen were at an advantage over their Nottingham associates because they received their London mail and newspapers by train whereas Nottingham depended on the mail coach. Numerous firms became established along the railway routes into the town bringing with them a 'big influx of Yorkshire and Tyneside men . . .regarded with suspicion by the old residents'.

From a population of 10,828 in 1801, the town grew to 32,741 in 1841 and 114,848 in 1901, but this growth was not parallelled by public service improvements. There had been little improvement in sanitary conditions, with frequent outbreaks of cholera usually traced to polluted water, and yet the Derby Infirmary had been

established in 1810, incidentally on the site of one of the town's water sources.

An official report of 1849 reveals that the drainage from cesspools and middens in some cases percolated through the walls of dwelling houses, while in some of the crowded courts in Walker Lane, Agard Street and Friar Gate there were cesspools emptied only once a year. This probably explains why the more affluent members of Derby society already lived outside the town in the villages of Quarndon, Duffield, Spondon and Ockbrook.

Pigot in 1835 wrote of Duffield 'It has long been esteemed a favourite residence of persons enjoying a respectable competence who prefer retirement and the quiet to the bustle of larger towns'. Improvements to the town came in the second half of the nineteenth century with the widening of St Peter's Street and Iron Gate, the removal of the Piazzas from the Market Head, and building of a second road bridge, Exeter Bridge, over the Derwent in 1850, and the

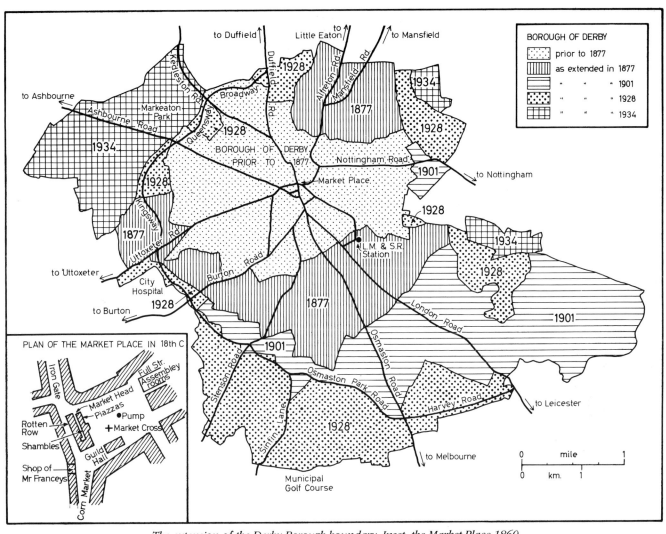

The extension of the Derby Borough boundary. Inset: the Market Place 1860.

building of the Temperance Hall, the Mechanics' Institute, Athenaeum (1839), built on the site of two coaching inns, and the Royal Drill Hall (1869). To serve the new suburbs, mill-buildings preceding housing, the churches of St Paul, Christ Church and Holy Trinity, and Nonconformist chapels were built.

The Arboretum, planned by James Loudon and largely financed by the Strutts, was opened in 1840, to be the first public park in the country, but at the beginning free access was limited. Its novelty attracted rail excursions from Sheffield and Leicester. Entertainment was available at the Theatre in Bold Lane — 'a small and convenient erection' — built in 1773 by James Augustus Whitley, and the new Assembly Rooms built in 1763, which replaced the original ones erected in 1714, and where concerts, lectures and balls were held. The Derby Town Museum and Library was established in 1871 and

the Central School of Art was opened in 1877.

The 1870s witnessed the formation of the Derbyshire Cricket Club, the transfer of horse-racing from Siddals Road (held on Sinfin Moor until 1803) to Nottingham Road, the building of the Alexandra Skating Rink and Bass's Free Baths on the Holmes. The first public baths and washhouse had been built in Full Street in 1858.

A private tramway system was started in 1880 which developed from the horse buses run since the arrival of the railways in 1840. The one route linked the Midland Railway Station with the new Friar Gate Station of the Great Northern Railway (1879). It enabled workers from the outlying built-up areas to reach the factories, many of which, such as Qualcast (1849), Fletchers (1860) and Leys (1874), had been built adjacent to the railways.

Electric street lighting was intro-

duced in 1893, some twelve years after Chesterfield, which with Guildford was first in the country. In 1907, Aiton and Company came to Derby from London, and Henry Royce arranged the transfer of the Rolls-Royce Company from Cook Street, Manchester, to the works erected by Handyside and Company in Nightingale Road. Rolls-Royce cars are no longer made in Derby, that activity having been transferred to Crewe in 1945. Another major employer which came to Derby in 1916 was the British Cellulose and Chemical Manufacturing Co Ltd later, as British Celanese, to merge with Courtaulds (1957) while in 1922, International Combustion Ltd commenced operations. The textile and smallware trade today is much less important than it was in the nineteenth and early twentieth centuries.

The town suffered little during either of the World Wars. In World War One, a Zeppelin brought con-

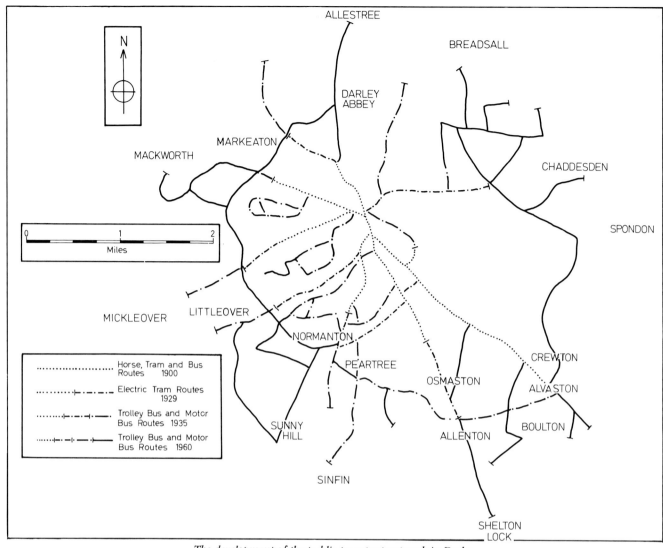

The development of the public transport network in Derby.

Derby Railway Station with tram and Shardlow and Castle Donington horse bus (c.1907).

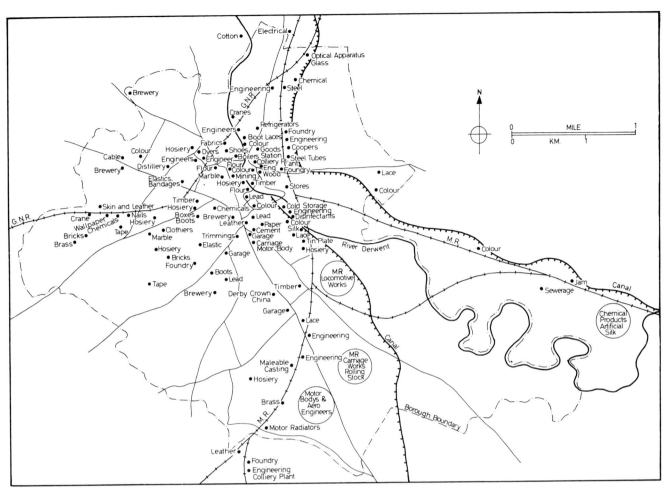

Derby's industries in the 1920s.

Derby in 1950, showing the site of Derventio (the Roman fort) with Strutt Park (right centre). The railway is the GNR (1878) resulting in the loss of Cherry Street, Short Street, Baxter Street and Short Street off Friar Gate with Granville Street and South Street cut short.

sternation to townfolk when it bombed Number-9 shed of the Railway Works, while in World War Two, Derby never suffered a 'terror' raid as did Coventry or Sheffield, the station being bombed in January 1941 and a lone German aircraft killed several people at the Rolls-Royce works in Nightingale Road in July 1942. Derbyshire experienced about two hundred air-raids in World War Two.

The present-day urban centres of population in Derbyshire mostly developed as route centres, many on hill-top sites and some at river crossings. Most received charters in the thirteenth and fourteenth centuries, giving them the right to hold markets and fairs, particularly Statute Fairs. Chesterfield, which was the site of a Roman fort, has been the second most important town and market centre in the County since the Middle Ages, although at the time of the Domesday Survey, it was part of the ancient demesne of Newbold. From the 1530s it was the chief market for lead and was a free

The River Derwent at Derby in the 1950s, looking upstream from Exeter Bridge with Electricity Station (1922), Silk Mill bell tower and Sowter's flour mill.

borough with two mills. Celia Fiennes (1697) saw ' coale pitts and quarraes of stone all about'. There were also iron works and potteries. The canal and the several railway companies brought further industrial development including a silk mill and several malthouses and breweries. In the late eighteenth century, Chesterfield miners were noted for their militancy.

Other mediaeval boroughs included Ashbourne, Castleton, Bakewell and Wirksworth. Ilkeston, Heanor, Glossop, Belper, Ripley, Sandiacre and Alfreton, which were early settlement sites and markets for the products of the surrounding area, grew rapidly during the middle and late nineteenth century in connection with the coal and iron industries, and also because of the textile industry. Buxton, Ilkeston and Glossop gained Borough status in the late nineteenth and early twentieth centuries. In the 1830s and 1840s, Ilkeston had aspirations, as had other places like Quarndon and Moira, towards spa status, with a new bath opened in 1830 — but these were shortlived. On the other hand, Buxton's early

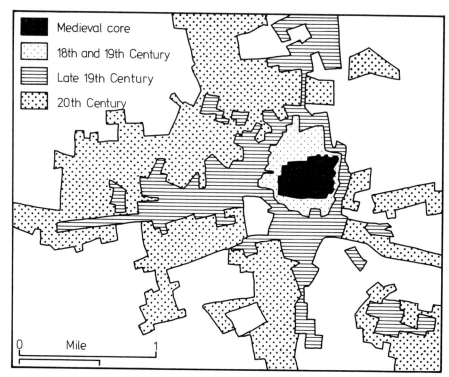

growth, particularly from the sixteenth century, was associated with its spa and promoted by the Devonshires in the eighteenth century, became the focus of society during the 'season'. Matlock Bath came to the fore as a spa town in the eighteenth century following the discovery

Key:
- Medieval core
- 18th and 19th Century
- Late 19th Century
- 20th Century

0   Mile   1

The development of Chesterfield.
Chesterfield's population growth
1664 1,500 (estimated)
1788 3,626
1801 4,267
1831 5,775
1851 7,101
1871 11,427
1891 13,242
1901 27,185 (extended boundary)
1981 72,767

The 'bottom' terminus of the cable railway at Matlock.

View of Ilkeston looking west, showing the Midland Railway's Town Station (1930s).

of warm springs in 1698, bottled Spa(w) water being delivered in Derby in 1732 at twopence per quart.

As inland spas, neither Matlock nor Buxton was important until the nineteenth century, when the railways were responsible for moving large numbers of people, particularly on Bank Holidays. Bradbury wrote in 1879 'to assert that Matlock Bath is crowded on Good Friday is really to extenuate circumstances . . . Rudely aroused on the buniferous day from her winter's rest, Matlock received visitors from half-a-dozen counties'. The practice of hydropathy on Matlock Bank by Ralph Davis, and its development by John Smedley and others in the latter part of the nineteenth century, gave a further boost to the town's growth, although the Bath and the Town did not always see 'eye to eye'.

Bath Street, Ilkeston, (c.1910) with the Rutland Hotel (right) adjacent to site of the Bath House. (originally erected 1830).

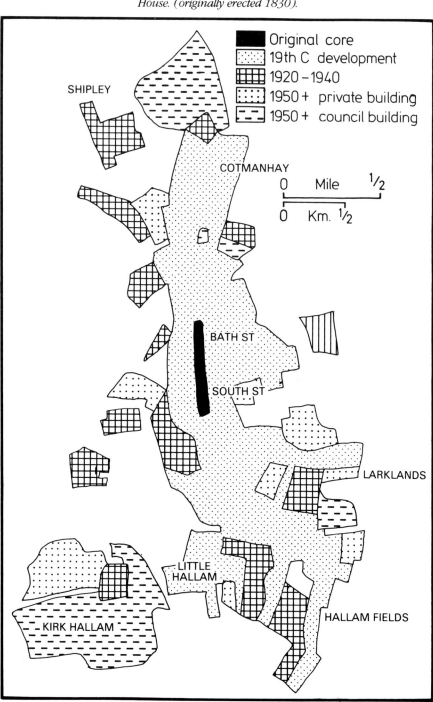

The development of Ilkeston and population growth.

1660 c.450
1801 2,422
1831 4,446
1851 6,122
1871 9,662
1891 19,744
1901 25,384
1981 34,573

Countryside

DURING the eighteenth century far-reaching changes took place in the landscape. Visitors to the County in the seventeenth and eighteenth centuries admired the splendour of the many country houses. Christopher Saxton marked thirty-two parks on his seventeenth century map, while Lysons listed fifty-four deer parks in 1817.

Defoe wrote of Chatsworth in the first decade of the eighteenth century, before its landscaping by Lancelot Brown '. . .it is indeed a palace for a prince, a most magnificent build-

ing, and, in spite of all the difficulties and disadvantages of situation is a perfect beauty . . .' During the eighteenth century the parks of the country houses were improved, as for example by Repton at Wingerworth and by Eames at Locko and Markeaton, and extended by sometimes engrossing the common pastures as on Derby Hills near Melbourne; cornfields disappeared and 'offensive' villages were removed as at Sudbury, Kedleston and Chatsworth, but visitors to the County still tended to be over-awed by the forbidding Peak.

In 1697/8, Celia Fiennes wrote: 'All

Derbyshire is full of steep hills and nothing but the peaks of hills . . . which makes travelling tedious and the miles long, you see neither hedge nor tree but only low dry stone walls round some ground . . .'

Open field agriculture, employing the strip method of cultivating arable, was still the pattern of husbandry in the lower lying part of the County with considerable areas of enclosure having already taken place, possibly starting with the erection of hurdles in the open-fields, as at Church Broughton in the seventeenth century. The enclosure of

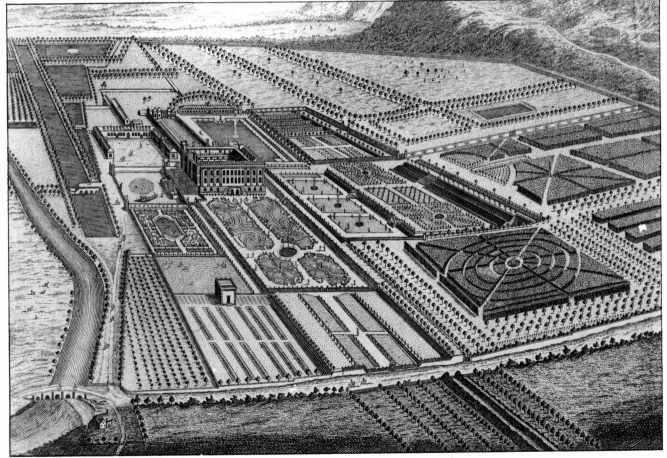

Chatsworth as seen by Kyp before Capability Brown's changes.

land gained momentum in the eighteenth century.

The first enclosure act in the County was for the parish of Scarcliffe and Palterton in 1730, followed by Shardlow in 1758. In the latter case, the enclosure resulted in the re-routing of the Loughborough-Derby turnpike road through the grounds at the rear of the Hall and the construction of new access roads. By the early 1800s most parishes had been enclosed, with Wyatt and Outram, in many instances, acting as the Commissioners. Generally speaking, the land was apportioned fairly between the original strip-owners, but the cost of fencing the enclosures tended to work against the small landowner, forcing him to sell his land. The enclosures resulted in consolidated landholdings, and led to the building of farms in the midst of the farmland, this leading to a partial dispersal of villages. The new roads created by the enclosure Commissioners were straight, as are the ones across Etwall Common and Spondon Moor, and they were often wide to accommodate the droves of animals on their way to market. The commutation of tithes in the 1830-40 period cleared another impediment to the improvement of agriculture.

Derbyshire has always been a backward County agriculturally, because of the climate, and the nature of the soil, although Arthur Young found it rather less backward than he had expected when he toured the North of England in 1770. He did, however, criticise the farmers around Derby who had enclosed their land, but who still used old methods, such as allowing their fields to lie fallow as in the old rotation system, and the use of ox for ploughing. This pattern of fallowing continued into the late nineteenth century. There was little innovation, although Mr Kendal of the Peacock Inn near Alfreton and the Duke of Devonshire, who at one time or another owned 14 per cent of Derbyshire, received praise for their work. Philip Kinder recorded the growing of camomile at Ashover, Morton, Shirland, North and South Wingfield. Combining farming with mining on the limestone inhibited improvement.

Sudbury Hall, the home of the Vernons.

Tissington, a closed village where the enclosure would be straightforward, there being only one landowner.

Towards the end of the century, the Board of Agriculture requested a number of County Reports, that for Derbyshire being prepared by Thomas Brown. He commented on the quantity of oats that were grown, 'because they were a hardy crop necessary in this climate'. Travelling north from Ashbourne he found it an 'overcoat colder' by the time he got to the top of Bentley Hill; he was snowed up at Newhaven for several days and forced to live on oatcakes, the staple foodstuff of the Peak, because bread was unobtainable.

A much more informative study was made twenty years later by John Farey, agent to the Duke of Bedford. He commented in particular on the efficient farming of industrialists such as the Strutts, the Arkwrights, Samuel Oldnow of Mellor, Mundy of Shipley, Oakes of Riddings and the Wrights of Butterley. Oldknow's gardener delivered vegetables and fruit to the cotton mill workpeople and tenants, the mill-agent deducting monies from their wages. At this time three-fifths of the County was under grass and only one-fifth was arable, so that Derbyshire farmers did not suffer quite as badly as other parts of the country in the slump following the Napoleonic Wars, although William Smith, who lived at Swarkestone Lowes, in his evidence to a Select Committee on Agriculture in 1833, claimed that he could not afford

The skeleton of the post-mill at South Normanton, now dismantled.   *The remains of the post-mill at Mapperley, Ilkeston, c.1900.*

'a pig, or kids' clothing'. Perhaps this was partly due to the increase in the County rate in part caused by the building of the new gaol and the County Hall. John Jephson Rowley in his prize report to the Royal Agricultural Society of England (1853) wrote that bones were used as manure in the Pleasley area about 1800. William Smith could not afford to use bones!

In the north-west of the County the white-faced woodland sheep was the main stock reared, while the County was important for the breeding of horses. Gaz wrote in 1831: 'Derbyshire had been long famous for its horses, ranking next to Leicestershire for its stout bony, clean-legged breed of work-horses which were principally black in colour'. Salop and Staffordshire dealers traded their smaller horses for the larger Derbyshire animals at the Derby or Pentrich Horse Fairs, which had been important since before the Civil War.

Cheese was an important farm product, particularly around Shottle and Aldwark and Hartshorne and remained important until American factory-produced cheeses captured the market in the 1860s, some ten thousand tons being produced each year. The first cheese factory in England was opened at Longford in 1870, and was followed by others at Brailsford, Grange Mill, Eggington and Hartington.

Kinder reported in 1817 that milk was being sent to Sheffield from Beighton, Eckington and Norton in barrels slung across horses and asses. This trade expanded with the building of the railways, so that in 1897 Derbyshire farmers from the Ashbourne-Buxton area paid a London agent to sell their milk direct to retailers. The Midland Railway served the large Express Dairy at Rowsley, and Henry Hill of Horsley sent milk to Sheffield daily from Kilburn Station. The supply of piped water to the limestone uplands in the 1960s resulted in a rapid increase in the number of dairy cattle.

A feature of the eighteenth century landscape was the windmill, the postmill as at West Hallam, Shardlow, South Normanton, Carsington, Norton, Chesterfield and Mapperley, and later the tower mill as at Heage, Ashbourne, Melbourne, and Riddings. Post mills date from before the fifteenth century. There were horse-driven mills for winnowing floors at Etwall and Ockbrook or for driving silk or cotton mills at Derby, Long-

stone or Belper. Corn-milling until the early nineteenth century, when steam-driven roller mills were introduced, was largely carried out in water-mills. In the Domesday Survey of 1086, some fifty mills were listed, many of them probably horizontal 'click' wheels, and this number had increased to over 160 by 1700.

Early corn mill sites are to be seen at Norbury, Melbourne and Grange Mill, but most of the present-day buildings date from the eighteenth and nineteenth centuries. Examples can be seen at Chatsworth Park Mill, Cauldwell's Mill at Rowsley, Smalley, South Wingfield, Milltown, Alport, Ashford, Cromford, Bradbourne, Bakewell and Longford. Henry Hill, who farmed Slackfields Farm at Horsley during the last quarter of the nineteenth century, used his father's watermill at Higham, his father-in-law's at Lea, as well as those at Coxbench, Darley, Milford and Pentrich. He also used the windmill at Kilburn.

The exploitation of the power potential of a small stream can be seen in Lumsdale at Matlock and in the Via Gellia, while there were more than twenty mills at one time or another on the Wye between Buxton

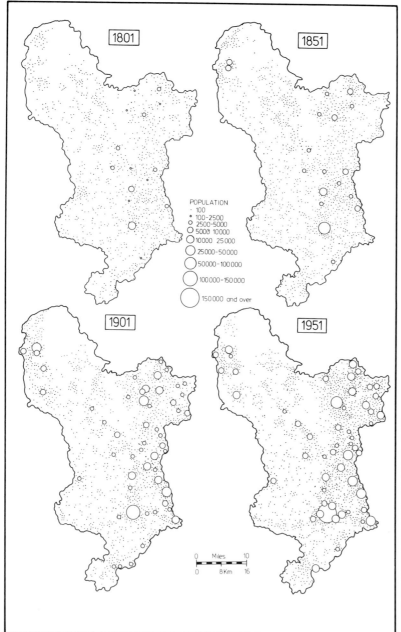

POPULATION

· 100
· 100–2500
○ 2500–5000
○ 5000–10000
○ 10000–25000
○ 25000–50000
○ 50000–100000
○ 100000–150000
○ 150000 and over

The distribution of the population — 1801-1951.

The stocks — at Eyam — would be used for punishing wrong-doers in the village. Behind is the early seventeenth-century Eyam Hall.

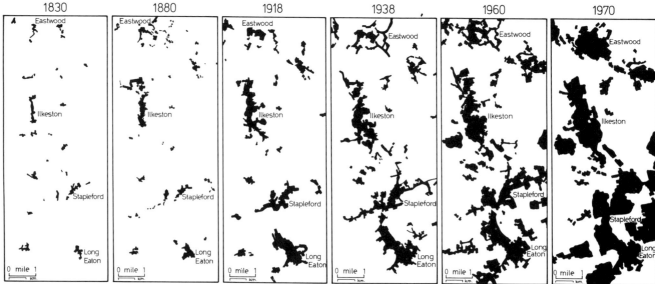

The urbanisation of population (1830-1970) along the Derbyshirte-Nottinghamshire boundary.

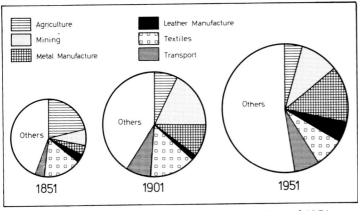

The changing pattern of employment between 1851 and 1951.

The lock-up and pinfold at Sandiacre. The pinfold was used for stray animals, the owner having to pay for their keep and release.

and Bakewell, and thirty mills with fifty-three wheels on the Derwent between Cromford and Derwent Mouth in the late eighteenth century. As well as corn mills, there were textile mills, bobbin-making mills, comb-making, slitting and mineral grinding mills for the manufacture of paint in these valleys.

During the late eighteenth and nineteenth centuries, there were significant changes in the distribution of population brought about by the exploitation of coal and the rapid growth of industrialisation. The domestic framework-knitting industry and weaving was well-established in the County south and east of Matlock, and the water-powered cotton-mills built in the Derwent Valley and along its tributaries, and in the north-west, brought about an increase in the population in these areas by providing work for females and children, and in some instances for unemployed lead-miners. The latter moved eastwards on to the developing coalfield on the Derbyshire-Nottinghamshire border. Little is known of the demographic effects of the Acts of Parliament at the turn of the century which resulted in the enclosure of the open common, arable and pasture lands where these still existed, but of the population of 161,142 recorded in the 1801 census, over half lived in communities of under a thousand persons, and most were dependent upon agriculture for a living. During the first twenty years of the nineteenth century, the population of the County

grew by about a third, growth being slowest in the agricultural lowlands and in the upland areas but rural depopulation was not yet a feature of the County demography.

Between 1821 and 1841, the settlements on the coalfield showed above average increases, while the rural areas showed declines. It is possible that the implementation of the new Poor Law in 1834 speeded up migration from agricultural to the established mining and manufacturing areas. The building of the North Midland Railway, and associated coal exploitation, resulted in rapid population growth in the north-east of the County, much of this coming from immigration. Clay Cross grew from 564 inhabitants in 1831 to 7,143 in 1891, Tunnel Terrace being the first new housing. Similar growth was found in the Swadlincote area.

Villages which were almost wholly dependent on the hosiery trade were almost stagnant, and after the 1830s experienced a loss of population. Between 1841 and 1861, although population kept pace with the national average, the County was losing people by emigration. Rural depopulation in the last quarter of the nineteenth century was widespread with areas adjacent to the urban centres showing vast increases. Litchurch, Derby's railway suburb, developed in the 1850s; the Glossop area expanded while Mellor declined, and the Derwent Valley towns showed stagnation and even decline.

The pattern of local government which was based on the parish unit

could no longer cope with these fluctuating demands, particularly where rapid population growth occurred. During the eighteenth century, the parish was responsible for the maintenance of the roads, the care of the poor, for those without work or who were indigent, and for maintaining law and order, all these functions being carried out by unpaid officials under the oversight of the Justices of the Peace at the Quarter Sessions. Ne'er-do-wells guilty of minor offences were usually placed in one of the houses of correction at Derby, Chesterfield, Ashbourne, Wirksworth or Tideswell, the miscreant being taken there from the village lock-up by the parish constable. Many who found their way into such places were poor folk, who were so placed as a result of punitive aspects of the Elizabethan Poor Laws and subsequent legislation.

The Workhouse or General Act of 1722/3 encouraged the creation of the parish workhouse as an alternative to out-relief and Gilbert's Act of 1782 facilitated the creation of voluntary Poor Law Unions, whereby parishes combined to fund a single workhouse. Some parish workhouses provided under the 1732 Act were used by several parishes, that at Dale Abbey, built in 1738, being used by a number of parishes in the Ilkeston area. This had the effect of compelling 'great numbers of lazy people, rather than submit themselves to the workhouse . . .to throw off the mask and maintain themselves'.

Similar workhouses were built at

Tissington in 1753, at Winster in 1774, and at Ashover, where forty-two parishes combined to buy a building originally built as a bath-house, adapting it as a workhouse, the institution being eloquently described by Farey. Not all workhouses were a success. The Dale workhouse was pulled down in 1779 because it was 'uninhabited' and every parish was 'sick of sending boarders to the house and repent the money spent on it'.

The practice of establishing joint workhouses was followed at Rosliston in 1802 and at Shardlow in 1811, when the 'township of Shardlow and parishes of Draycott, Sawley and Worthington resolved to build a Poor House' at a cost of £1,200. By 1814, twenty-four other parishes had joined, but very soon the parish of Shepshed was unwilling to spend money on transporting its poor so far. In Derby, the parishes of St Alkmund, All Saints, St Peter's and St Werburgh's built their own workhouses and in 1811, Farey wrote that there were thirty workhouses in the County, of which twenty-two were for single parishes or townships. He described them 'as good, or perhaps rather better than in the surrounding counties . . .Few able persons seemed to be unemployed, except during temporary stagnations of the manufactories'. Sir Philip Eden also commented favourably in his *State of the Poor* written in 1797, recording that the twenty-eight poor in Chesterfield were partly maintained at home and partly in the workhouse. At Wirksworth, the children were instructed in the catechism and reading, and the inmates' food consisted of oat bread, no beer or cheese except at Christmas, and water potage, which was oatmeal and a small onion boiled with water. Initially the workhouse had the desired effect of reducing the poor rates, but these were not particularly low in townships or in parishes where there were cotton mills, which relied on apprentice labour.

Following the Napoleonic Wars, when many men were out of work, the poor rate doubled. However, able-bodied men were refused relief, and work such as spinning, cobbling and framework-knitting was found for

them, and this helped to reduce the rates. Following the Act of 1834, the administration of the Poor Law was changed, so that thereafter Derbyshire was divided into nine union districts, each with its workhouse.

Law and order in the eighteenth and early nineteenth centuries were also the responsibility of the parish through its parish constables, who were backed up by the local justice, and if necessary, the militia. To cope with the increasing disorder before and after the Napoleonic Wars, a large number of lock-ups were built in villages and towns in the last quarter of the eighteenth century, there being 118 recorded in a Return of 1790. As Sir Robert Peel said in the House of Commons on 15 April 1829, "Each parish was quite isolated as far as prevention of crime was concerned from each other."

To supplement the system, Associations for the Prosecution of Felons were formed which offered cash incentives for the arrest of miscreants. The South Wingfield Association had thirty-three members in 1789 covering the area of Alfreton, Pentrich, Crich, Codnor Park, Toadhole and South Wingfield.

However, when the question of a County Police Force was raised in 1839, it was generally felt that the current system of control was adequate, although two more lock-ups were later built at Chapel-en-le-Frith in 1843 and at Alfreton in 1844. The mill-owners, who had their own militia, spoke out against a County Police Force but this may have been because of the need to raise a Police Rate. They did, however, echo the sentiments of the County populace who held many protest meetings. The County Police was eventually established following the compulsory order of he 1856 Police Act, the force initially consisting of 156 men distributed throughout the County whose main base was at Belper. In 1888 the control of this force passed from the Quarter Sessions to a Standing Joint Committee consisting of County Councillors and magistrates and it was subject to inspection by inspectors appointed by the Home Office as was the earlier constabulary.

The nineteenth century saw education evolving from the ideals of

charitable benevolence which still survived from the Georgian Age, to the Forster Act of 1870, which propounded the principle that education was the right of the citizen and not the by-product of patronage, or an adjunct to the earning of a living.

In 1800 there were some seventy-four schools in the County provided by parish charities. These schools traditionally included a schoolroom and a house for the teacher. The school at Norbury was built alongside the road on waste land; the schoolmaster at Church Broughton had to build his own house, and Mugginton School was a barn on the glebe land! Indoctrination of the principles of the Church of England was frequently the main objective, and as at Mickleover 'to teach poor children to read and write and that the schoolmaster should attend to their morals'.

The fear that an educated poor would lead to anarchy was allayed by the teaching of reading 'for the sake of reading the Bible, writing, together with morals, and arithmetic, with piety', thus preparing children for 'their station in life and their place in heaven'. Sunday schools were set up, usually by industrial benefactors like Arkwright in 1785, or by the village, as at Flagg in 1789, where there were fifty attenders.

Charity however was not enough, so that in 1833 Parliament approved a sum not exceeding £20,000 to aid private subscriptions for the erection of school houses for the education of the children of the poorer classes in Great Britain, but the grant was only available, if at least half of the estimated cost had been raised by local voluntary subscription. Two voluntary societies used this money: the Nonconformist, British and Foreign, which was formerly the Lancastrian Society, and the National Society, which had been established 'for promoting the education of the poor in the principles of the Church of England'.

Some of the charity schools which had connections with the established church became National schools, 'by virtue of the local vicar taking over a crumbling foundation'. Melbourne was such a school, having been endowed in 1738. The vicar applied

The Overseers of Alfreton in 1909 attempted to raise money to preserve this 'extremely rare' building — the House of Confinement (1844).

Melbourne Junior School, Penn Lane. Cast-iron gothic style windows possibly from Weatherhead and Glover, Derby.

for a National Society grant in 1822, claiming 170 boys and 150 girls were in a fair way to becoming 'as turbulent members of the community if left to themselves, as their parents'. Mr Bagge, the curate, who took responsibility for the school following the vicar's illness, had the school built before the subscriptions had been assured. He received the National Society's grant, contrary to the rules, received a reprimand from the Bishop and a loss of £158 5s 0d (£158.25) from his salary, which was put towards the cost of the school.

Grants for fabric were one thing, running costs were another. Children paid fees, frequently double if of the 'other persuasion'. Alvaston and Boulton Church of England School took 20 children for one penny a week under Gilbert's Charity, and also children of poor parents who paid twopence a week, while others paid threepence or fourpence. The British Society's schools were particularly strong in the Belper area where the Strutts were influential. William Strutt had incorporated a school in the attic room of his North Mill at Belper, and Samuel Oldnow appointed a teacher at his Mellor Mill in 1801, but they were for Saturday schooling.

Schools were also supported by the rural gentry. Lady Harrington paid all the fees of the children attending Elvaston School, as did the Duke of Portland at Whitwell, the Duke of Devonshire at Pentrich, while Lord Vernon and the rector shared the payment of fees for the children attending Sudbury School. The Drury-Lowes supported the school at Denby and W.E.Nightingale built the school at Lea.

Schools were also provided by industrialists, like Walter Evans at Darley Abbey, who furthered the education of employees' children. Peter Arkwright supported the schools at Cressbrook, while the Butterley Company provided schools at Codnor Park, Ironville in 1841, Riddings and Ripley, the Clay Cross Company at Clay Cross in 1843, the Staveley Company at Barrow Hill in 1856 and Thomas Firth and Sons at New Whittington in 1861. Other schools were established by subscription like that at Shardlow in 1811, while dame schools abounded, ranging from childminding 'academies' to places where the three R's were taught. An inspector to such a school might find the only books used being 'the miracles and parables of our Lord and a few torn and tattered Bibles'. There were many private schools which taught surveying, book-keeping, languages (for young ladies), etc.

The death knell of this archaic system was sounded by W.E.Forster's 1870 Education Act which aimed to bring education within the reach of every English home. A survey of school places in each parish was carried out and voluntary bodies were given six months' grace to fill the deficiencies. If they failed to do so, a School Board was to be elected with the authority to build and run a school, to levy rates for the building and its maintenance, to help poor children with their fees, and to make school attendance compulsory, though few boards in fact exercised this power. Derbyshire soon experienced the effect of this new measure. Within a year, six school boards were operating in the County and by 1875 there were twelve — at Bradwell, Chesterfield, Clay Lane United (Clay Cross), Dronfield, Eckington, Foston and Scropton, Long Eaton, Norton, Shirland and Higham, South Wingfield, Unstone, as well as in Derby. The elections to the School Boards provided an opportunity for the various sectarian bodies to promote their respective candidates, the block vote being used effecively by the Roman Catholics in Derby, where in 1892 the Derby Trades Council secured two seats. Interdenominational strife between Church and Chapel was fierce. In 1883, at Crich, partisanship reached the level of farce with nocturnal 'battles' with posters and paste between the Anglican and Nonconformist supporters, both having their own schools. The threat of a common enemy in the form of the Dethick Lea and Holloway School Board did not assuage the strife though a board school was eventually built. The School Boards handed over their responsibilities to the County and Borough Councils in 1902 when municipal education took over.

Before the Derbyshire County Council was constituted on 1 April 1889 following the Local Government Act of 1888, the administration of County affairs was largely in the hands of the magistrates who met quarterly in Quarter Sessions, to deal not only with persons committed for trial, but also to transact a considerable amount of administrative business. There were already in existence Boards of Guardians, who were concerned with the relief of the poor in the groups or 'unions' of parishes from which they were appointed, and Parliament had already recognised the right to certain boroughs created by Royal Charter or by Act of Parliament to govern their own internal affairs, as was the case with Derby and Chesterfield.

Until 1889, outside the boroughs the main unit of local administration was the parish acting in its civil capacity. In urban areas local boards of health could be set up under the Public Health Act of 1857 to deal with sanitary and sewerage matters, and from 1872 rural sanitary districts — based on the Poor Law Unions — could be set up in rural areas. Under the Highways Act of 1835, local highway boards could be set up to deal with highway matters. It was to rationalise the confusion which arose from these various bodies, which rarely coincided in the area they served, that the Act of 1888 was passed.

The County Council was vested with the powers which had previously been the prerogative of the Quarter Sessions, and these included the making and levying of a County Rate, the power to borrow money for County purposes, the control of County buildings and lunatic asylums, the establishment of reformatory and industrial schools, the control of main roads and bridges, the appointment and control of certain offices including the Treasurer, Surveyor and Analyst, and also the County Coroners, the enforcement of legislation with regard to the diseases of animals and to weights and measures, the execution of the Riot Act if necessary, and the registration of places of public worship and of scientific societies. The Quarter Sessions were left to deal with any appeals against the County Rate, and

functions previously their responsibility not transferred to the County Council.

A Standing Joint Committee, made up of members of the County Council and Justices of the Peace appointed by Quarter Sessions, was responsible for the control of the County Police, the appointment of a Clerk of the Peace, and of Clerks to the Justices in the different Petty Sessional Divisions into which the County was divided. New powers invested in the County Council included the prevention of pollution of rivers, the power of compulsory purchase, the promotion of and opposition to Bills of Parliament, the preparation of Bylaws for approval by Central Government and the appointment of a Medical Officer of Health.

Further powers included education, supervising midwives (1902), the collection of Road Fund Licences (1908), establishing institutions for the treatment of tuberculosis (1901), and for the care of the mentally deficient (1913), maternity and child welfare (1918), the general care and training of blind persons (1920), the setting up of the Local Land Charges Register (1925), the registration of births, marriages and deaths (1929), this last function being transferred from the Boards of Guardians, the Registration Districts which followed the boundaries of the existing Poor Law Unions, along with increasing responsbilities in connection with Public Health and Housing, including the control of ribbon building in 1935.

The first meeting of the Council was chaired by Sir Thomas William Evans of Allestree Hall, near Derby. He was succeeded by Sir Henry Wilmot, then by Lord Waterpark and Herbert Strutt, with James Oakes leading the Council through the years of World War One.

In 1894, local government saw the creation of the Parish Council, and the District Council of either the Urban or Rural District which often took over from a local board. The Parish Council was entrusted with certain local functions including the appointment of Overseers for Poor Law purposes, and it was empowered to undertake the duty of lighting the parish, providing baths, washhouses, burial grounds and play-grounds. It was also responsible for the roads until 1930 when the cost of maintaining the main highways passed to the County Council.

The Urban and Rural District Councils took over the responsiblity of the sanitary authorities. When the Boards of Guardians ceased to exist on 1 April 1930, the County Council's Public Assistance Committee became responsible for the workhouses.

The County Council exercised certain control over the different units of local government, but the County Borough of Derby was excluded from this. The units of local government which made up the area of the adminitrative County were the four Municipal Boroughs of Buxton, Chesterfield, Glossop and Ilkeston, over which the County Council exercised little control, the sixteen Urban Districts which were miniature versions of the boroughs and the nine Rural Districts which were subdivided into rural parishes. These units were altered in area and redefined in status from time to time as a consequnce of the 1929 Local Government Act. An example of this was the creation of the Urban District of Whaley Bridge in 1934.

Following Charles II's celebrated 'Indulgence' of 1672, which freed Nonconformists and Recusants from the existing penal laws which derived from Elizabethan statutes, nonconformist places of worship could be established. At the same time Quakers, who had been imprisoned on religious grounds, were released. Such a sweeping move resulted in a great outcry among more orthodox worshippers. Within twelve months the Indulgence was cancelled, but not before twenty-eight Presbyterian and eight Independent Ministers had been licensed in Derbyshire. As a result of the cancellation, Recusants and Nonconformists were once again illegal, and their activities were punishable at the County Assizes. In 1682, four hundred and fifty adult Roman Recusants were fined at Derby in one session of the Assizes, along with forty-seven Quakers and six Protestant Dissenters.

A further Declaration of Indulgence in 1686 resulted in a Roman Catholic chapel being built at North

St Thomas (1830/32), New Brampton. The chancel was added in 1891.

St Peter's (1824), Belper, was built at a cost of £12,000. The church authorities considered a provision of 1,800 places sufficient for a population of 6,000. There were five other denominations with chapels. The Weslyans had seating for 1,400 in their chapel in Chapel Street. Prior to 1824, Belper and Milford were in the parish of Duffield.

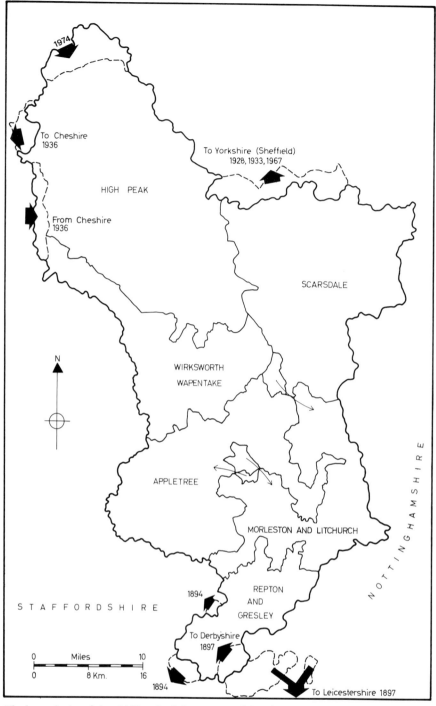

The boundaries of the old Hundred divisions, and the changes in the County's boundary.

Unitarians were specially exempted from the Act. At the Session of 1689, eighteen Protestant Dissenting Preachers took the oath and were duly licensed, sixteen of them being Presbyterians, this showing the hold that they had gained by this time over other forms of dissent in Derbyshire. The Presbyterians traced the strength of their position to the Parliament of 1644 which had set up provincial synods. At the same Translation Session of 1689, a large number of dissenting places of worship were registered, usually in dwelling-houses.

The Moravians established a church at Ockbrook, where a settlement developed, in 1750, some nine years after John Wesley had visited the village. In 1746, there were only seven Methodist Circuits — the fifth circuit being Yorkshire, which included both Nottinghamshire and Derbyshire. Wesley was to visit the County on numerous occasions; sometimes he was welcomed, at other times rejected, as on his first visit to Derby in March 1764, when he was forced to walk away because he could not make himself heard above the 'hallooing and shouting on every side'. On 25 March 1764, he preached in Crich, where the chapel which still stands was built the following year. His last visit to Derby was in July 1788 at the age of 85. He was travelling from Sheffield when the axle-tree of his chaise snapped and the carriage overturned. Wesley crept out of a window and obtained another chaise at the 'Peacock', Oakerthorpe, so keeping his preaching engagement in Derby that evening.

Attendance at church or chapel was poor except at Easter or Christmas. The curate of All Saints' Church, Sawley, wrote: 'On my first coming to Sawley in 1785 the congregation was small. Here was an Anabaptist Chapel which was now occupied by Methodists and another built for the Baptists. The old church-goers were most of them dead, and many of the younger people of the poor-sort especially are lured to one or both of these places . . .'

Sir George Crewe of Calke wrote of Ticknall (1846): '. . .on a Sabbath morning . . .he will see men or

Lees in Hathersage parish, and the chapels of the Hunlokes at Wingerworth and of the Eyres at Newbold were thrown open to corporate Mass. But this was again a short-lived Indulgence because, following James II's flight in 1688, Protestant mobs sacked the last two chapels. It was during James II's reign that the Roman Catholics, Fitzherbert of Norbury and Hunloke of Wingerworth, were made lieutenants of the County.

The Revolution of 1688, which was largely engineered by William Cavendish, later the first Duke of Devonshire, resulted in the Toleration Act the following year. This Act exempted Dissenters from the church — compelling ordinances of Elizabeth, providing they took an oath against papal rule and supremacy. Dissenting congregations had to register their place of worship before the bishop or the justices, and all dissenting ministers were required to accept the Articles of Religion at the Quarter Sessions. All Papists and woman idly lounging at their doors, or in the streets; boys and girls at play . . .some in their gardens or leaning over a pig-sty; and were he to enter the houses, very many would be found in bed . . .unconscious that it was Sunday.' Vicarages to let at Spondon and Egginton (1787) suggest absentee parsons, not encouraging church attendance.

The developing coalfield and textile settlements in the County were ill-provided with church accommodation and only a quarter of the existing seats were free. Many of the churches in the late eighteenth century were in bad repair, the ones at Barlow, Edale, Stapenhill and Kirk Hallam being in danger of falling down. Church Gresley and Measham churches had to be rebuilt.

It was Archbishop Butler in 1821 who urged an increased in the numbers of free seats, but by 1835, for an urban population of over 150,000, there were only 12,000 free seats. To increase seating capacities, churches built galleries, as was requested at Crich in 1772. New Commissioner type churches were built but the lack of accommodation led to the various Nonconformist bodies building chapels in the new-growing townships.

It also gave scope for new groups to establish themselves, such as the Primitive Methodist Connexion whose first meeting was held in May 1807 on Mow Cop. It was in Belper that their enthusiastic and noisy singing earned them the nickname 'Ranters'. Later in the century Smed-ley of Lea, where there was a chapel in the mill, introduced his brand of Nonconformity to the Ashover area. The incumbant of Sandicare parish in 1772 reported on the 'scandalous profanation of the Sabbath . . .by the Dippers . . .some hundreds were assembled at the side of a pond to see some of the people dipt in the water . . .'

As a result of all this, the Nonconformist Church in the nineteenth century filled many of the religious gaps in the newly developing areas. 'It is for the living church to create its own organisation and to modify it by retrenchment here and expansion there as new conditions arise and new needs have to be met'.

Modern Times

THERE have been many changes since the turn of the century, including a relocation of industry, a change in transport networks, the introduction of new agricultural practices, and the setting up of the Peak District National Park and the new local authorities.

Today, there are only three collieries operating in the County, and what accessible coal remains on the exposed coalfield is being gained by opencast methods. Colliery buildings have been demolished, pit heaps reshaped or planted with trees, and opencast sites landscaped, as is the case with the Shipley Park site. Iron ore has not been mined in any quantity in the County for over a century, and today neither pig iron nor wrought iron is produced. So has ended a period of industrial activity.

The spoil heaps and workings of the lead mines are being re-worked for fluorspar, barytes and lead concentrates, and when that work is done the landscape specialists move in, thereby destroying evidence of the past, but industrial buildings continue to intrude into the landscape as at Stanton, and the Lady Wash Mine for the sheer necessity of employment. In contrast to these contracting industries, the activities of the limestone producers have

The Peak District National Park symbol near Dovedale with Thorpe Cloud in the distance.

increased. The planners have a perennial struggle in their attempts to control the avaricious demands of the companies quarrying in the Peak District. The cement works between Hope and Bradwell is a monument to the twentieth century and the need to provide employment in a National Park. The demands for water have seen the flooding of valleys and therefore the past.

Equally intrusive into the landscape are the electricity power stations and the associated pylons built along the Trent Valley from Drakelow to Ratcliffe-on-Soar, and the gravel workings which move steadily westward along the Derwent and Trent Valleys. The old mill buildings of the Derwent Valley and elsewhere have found new uses, in the case of Cromford, exploiting its historical significance.

To counter the decline of industry on the coalfield, industrial estates have been created on derelict colliery sites at Tibshelf, Codnor, Pinxton, Ilkeston, Alfreton and Clay Cross. Today a wide variety of industries operate and they have stabilised the population. The Swadlincote area, where a pit heap has been adapted to a ski slope, has similar problems with the desmise of the coalfield, the gaping clay pits and derelict industrial sites.

The changing pattern of industry has seen an alteration in the communications system. The building of the M1 motorway in 1969 opened up an area which previously had no clearly defined north-south line of communication, and to some extent it offset the extensive railway closures that took place in the 1950s and 1960s. The M42 motorway has had a beneficial effect on South Derbyshire. The restructuring of the railway system has resulted in the obliteration of the once important Trent Junction, and the re-routing of services following the closure of the Matlock to Manchester line, has resulted in the diminution of Derby's importance as a railway centre, although it is still important for engine development and carriage building. Derby, along with Nottingham and Leicester and their respective counties, has been responsible for the development of the East Midlands Airport at Castle Donington as a replacement for the

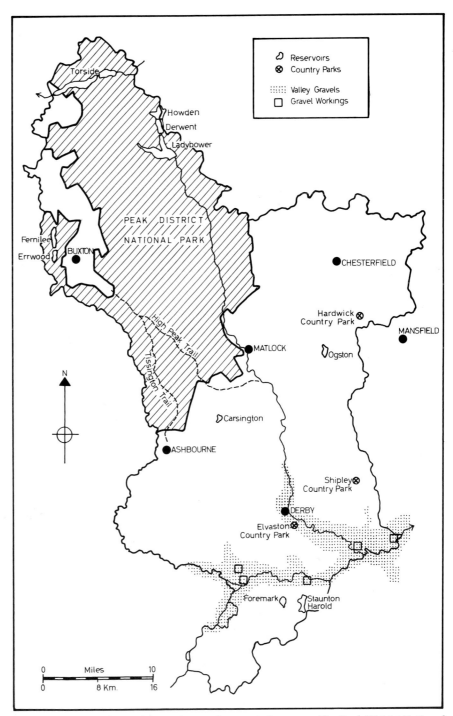

The changing landscape of Derbyshire in the twentieth century. The Peak District National Park (shaded) shows Buxton excluded because of limestone exploitation.

pre-war municipal aerodrome at Burnaston.

Changes have taken place in agriculture. Farms have increased in size, hedgerows have been uprooted to produce larger-sized fields for the convenience of machinery, broken stone-walls have been replaced by stake and wire, and mechanisation has resulted in an increase in the ploughing of upland pasture for improved grassland and crops. Oats and wheat have given way to barley, some of which is being grown in

upland fields at a height of a thousand feet (300 metres) above sea level. Hectares have been planted with conifers.

The decrease in the amount of labour employed on the land has resulted in a downward trend in the quantity of root crops grown. It is interesting that the acreage of arable land today is about the same as it was one hundred years ago, but twice what it was in 1930. Conversely, the labour force today is very much less than half of what it was in 1939.

The renovated and altered chapel resited at Carsington Reservoir, one of fifty in the County.

The Pennine Way, approaching Kinder Downfall — a leisure provision.

The ancient game of Shrovetide football, once played nationally but now only at Ashbourne, is a tourist attraction. The goals are mill sites on the Henmore Brook.

Smedley's Hydro, Matlock, built in the early 1850s. In 1867 the therapeutic establishment treated 2,000 patients and was one of nine establishments on Matlock Bank. Today the headquarters of Derbyshire County Council.

The Trent Valley near Repton showing meanders the river bluff and the changing course of the river.

It was in the 1930s that the Council for the Preservation of Rural England established its headquarters at Sheffield, with 'a special care' for the Peak. In the preface to *The Threat to the Peak* (1931), G.M.Trevelyan wrote 'The tide of public opinion is moving with great rapidity in the direction of a new demand for the preservation of natural beauty . . . Outrages possible today will be impossible twenty years hence . . .' An indirect result of this was that in 1951 the first British National Park was created: the Peak District National Park. It is surrounded by urban areas with a total population of nearly 18,000,000 people, and is accessible to many more by way of the M1 and the M62. The village of Edale, which has a weekday population of about 360, has to cater for more than ten times that number at summer weekends.

The pressures on the Peak District landscape is increasing annually and, to offset this, cars are banned from the Goyt Valley at weekends. Country parks have been created, the first established in Derbyshire being in 1970 at Elvaston Castle, previously the home of the Stanhope family and one of the homes of the Earls of Harrington. The second, with its funpark addition, is at Shipley, the estate of the Mundy family.

The centre of County administration was moved from Derby to the more central location of Matlock in 1955, and in 1977 the enlarged County Borough of Derby was granted city status fifty years after the creation of the Diocese of Derby.

The reorganisation of local government in 1974 resulted in only minor alterations in the County boundary, the addition of Tintwistle RDC extending it in the north-west.

In the past the boundaries of Derbyshire have been altered from time to time, along the valley of the Goyt, in the north-east where the city of Sheffield encroaches onto the moorland, and in the south where part of the County was separated by a part of Leicestershire until the late nineteenth century. As a result of the redrawing of these boundaries in 1897, parts of Leicestershire came into Derbyshire and vice versa. But none of these changes has altered the essential character of Derbyshire, a County which links lowland and highland England, although the north-west has closer affinities with the Manchester conurbation as the north-east has with Sheffield.

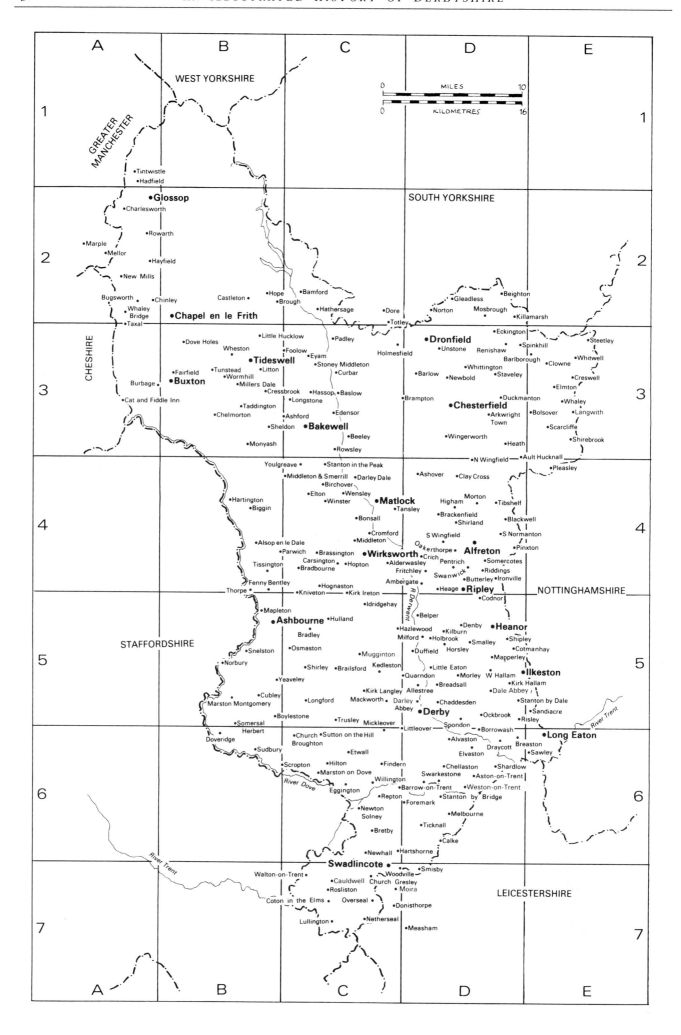

Suggested Reading

To put Derbyshire into its regional context, reference should be made to J.V.Beckett's *The East Midlands from A.D. 1000* (1988), G.H.Dury's *The East Midlands and the Peak* (1963), P.Staffords *The East Midlands in the Early Middle Ages* (1985) and M.Palmer's and P.Neveson's *Industrial Landscapes of the East Midlands* (1992).

F.Wolverson Cope's *Geology Explained in the Peak District* (1976) and P.R.Rodgers *Derbyshire Geology* (1977) give the rock formations and structure, with N.Pevsner's and E.Williamson's *Derbyshire* volume in *The Buildings of England* series (1979) and B.Hutton's *Historic Farmhouses around Derby* (1990) covering the main building types.

For aspects of the history of the County, and for Archaeology in particular, reference should be made to the *Derbyshire Archaeological Society Journal*, and *The Derbyshire Miscellany*.

Also of interest are J.Barnatt's *The henges, stone circles and ring cairns of the Peak District* (1990), H.C.Lane's *The Romans in Derbyshire* (1986), M.Brassington's *Roman Derby* (1991) in conjunction with the *Derbyshire Archaeological Society Journal* Volume CV (1985). R.Hodge's *Wall to Wall History* (1991) describes the many aspects of history to be discovered in the vicinity of Roystone Grange, and D.Roffe's *The Derbyshire Domesday* (1986) clarifies some of the mysteries of the survey.

The county's gentry and their houses are covered in M.Craven's *A Derbyshire Armory* (1991), M.Craven's and M.Stanley's *The Derbyshire Country House* (1991) which is a follow-up to their two volumes under the same title. More specific is S.M.Wright's *The Derbyshire Gentry and the Fifteenth Century* (1983), T.Brighton's *Royalists and Roundheads in Derbyshire* (1981), B.Stone's *Derbyshire in the Civil War* (1992) and L.E.Simpson's *Derby and the Forty-Five* (1933).

The county's industrial past is detailed in F.Nixon's *Industrial Archaeology of Derbyshire* (1969) and H.Harris's *Industrial Archaeology of the Peak District* (1971) used in conjunction with *Derbyshire Industrial Archaeology Gazetteer of sites for the Boroughs of the High Peak* (1984), *Erewash* (1986), and *Amber Valley* (1992). Recent publications dealing with particular aspects of the county's industrial history are R.Christian's *Butterley Brick* (1990), S.Dunkerley's *Robert Bakewell* (1988), P.Riden's *Gazeteer of Charcoal Blast Furnaces* (1988), C.C.Owen's *The Leicestershire & South Derbyshire Coalfield, 1200-1900* (1984) and D.T.Kiernan's *The Derbyshire Lead Industry in the Sixteenth Century* (1989). The lead industry is covered in detail in the Bulletins of the Peak District Mine Historical Society. C.Hadfield's *Canals of the East Midlands* (1966) has been added to by the individual studies of P.Stevenson *The Nutbrook Canal* (1970), C.Richardson's *The Waterways Revolution (1992)* and C.Swainson's *Waterways to Derby* (1993). R.Le Leux's *The East Midlands* Volume IX in *A Regional History of the Railways of Great Britain* (1984) has been added to by P.Stevenson's (ed) *Midland Counties Railway* (1989), M.Higginson's *The Friargate Line* (1989) and Grafton and Band's *The Ashover Light Railway* (1989). These with Dodd and Dodd's *Peakland Roads and Trackways* (1980) should be read in association with B.Travers's *Trading Patterns in the East Midlands* in *Midland History XV* (1990).

Townscapes have been covered by Barracuda Books: Glossop, Chesterfield, Buxton, Long Eaton and Derby, but the history of Chesterfield has been covered in greater detail by J.Beastall, P.Riden and D.Fowkes (1974-1984), Derby by M.Craven (1988) and Georgian Ashbourne (1989 and 1991) edited by A.Henstock.

Various journals give an insight into particular times and places: *The Diary of Joseph Jenkinson of Dronfield 1833-43* ed. K.Battye (1987), *The Autobiography of Leonard Wheatcroft of Ashover 1627-1706* ed. D.Riden, in *A Seventeenth Century Scarsdale Miscellany* (1993), *The Diaries of Henry Hill 1872-1896* ed J.Heath (1982) and *The Diary of George Mushet 1805-1813* ed R.Healey (1982).

Local History groups at Bakewell, Belper, Chellaston, Clifton, Dethick, Lea and Holloway, Hartington, Hartshorne, Hayfield, Heanor, Ilkeston, Longstone, New Mills, Ockbrook and Borrowash, Renishaw, Repton, Spondon, Ticknall, Weston-on-Trent and Whitwell, have at one time or another, produced informative monographs, and trails such as the Cresswell Archaeological Way and the Roystone Grange Trail as well as those produced by the Derby Museums Service and the Arkwright Society all add to the local picture.

Index

Figures in *italics* refer to illustrations
Letters and figures in brackets refer to the key map.